Karen Davis

You Might As Well Laugh at . . .

. . . lanyards kids make at camp—and insist you wear

. . . Halloween candy syndrome, or how to keep Necco wafers and Raisinettes from being your toddler's breakfast

. . . sock bumps, the mysterious painful lumps in socks only kids feel

. . . February, the month when it's too cold, too difficult and too much trouble to stay sane

. . . missing objects, or how a wallet ends up as Barbie's sleeping bag

. . . recreating an exploding volcano out of cornstarch

. . . and the moment the most enlightened parent finally yells, "Because I said so!"

"A storyteller with contagious wit."
            —Mary Kay Blakely, author of _American Mom_

"A joy ride from the pandemonium of new motherhood to the poignancy of high school graduation."
            —Carol Weston, author of _Girltalk_

You might as well laugh...

because crying will only smear your mascara

sandi kahn shelton

St. Martin's Paperbacks

Published by arrangement with Bancroft Press.

YOU MIGHT AS WELL LAUGH

Library of Congress Catalog Number: 96-86486

ISBN: 0-312-96976-7

Printed in the United States of America

Bancroft Press hardcover edition 1997
St. Martin's Paperbacks edition/April 1999

St. Martin's Paperbacks are published by St. Martin's Press, 175 Fifth Avenue, New York, NY 10010.

10 9 8 7 6 5 4 3 2 1

To Jimbo, whose love has sustained me, and Ben, Allie and Stephanie, who not only make me laugh, but let me put their childhoods in the paper each week

And to the memory of Nan, whose laughter lives in my heart

Acknowledgments

It may take a village to raise a child, but it takes an entire metropolitan area to get a humor column into the paper every week, into the magazine once a month, and then into a book. I've been lucky. I've had plenty of help and advice.

Thanks especially to Alice Mattison, who not only can think up column topics an hour before deadline, but doesn't mind being called on the phone and having columns read to her in a voice filled with hysteria. Through the 20 years of our friendship, she's given me love, encouragement, child care, and meals to keep me going.

And thanks to Diane Cyr, who lets me write about her life more often than she's probably aware, especially now that she moved out of town and doesn't get the paper anymore. Only once has she called to tell me something and started with, "Now this is off the record!"

Thanks and peace to the Monday Morning Yoga Class and Lunch Club (Bobbi Harshav, Rhoda Rosenfeld, Cecilia Moffett, Dru Nadler, and Alan Franzi), who instinctively understand that writers need the quiet of yoga, and then immediately afterwards some bacon, eggs, and heated political debate to help them get back to the Real World of Writing.

Many thanks to Judsen Culbreth, editor of *WorkingMother* magazine, who first thought these columns should be in a collection; and to *WorkingMother*'s Mary McLaughlin, the finest line editor, friend, and lunch partner anyone could have. Susan Seliger, former deputy editor of the magazine, has my undying gratitude for her astonishing phone call telling me she was buying my first three columns.

Bushels of thanks go to Mary Kittredge and Kathleen Kudlinski, fellow writers who get together with me once a week to exchange ideas and horror stories, and who more than once have supplied paper, pens, and pep talks.

And to Rick Sandella, the features editor at the *New Haven Register*, who has always let me write just what I wanted and who almost never complains when it's late because of some household disaster that he knows I'll write about next week.

Also thanks to *Register* publisher Bill Rush, who inherited both me and the column when he took on his jobs, and who was the first to say "Congratulations" when the column was named Best Column in New England. And to Dave Butler, the former *Register* editor, for always saving my space.

And of course, lots of love and gratitude to my parents: my late father, Charles Myers, and my mother, Joan Graham, for teaching me that you're really better off laughing when the roof is caving in and something's boiling over on the stove; to my stepmother, Helen Myers, who more than once has reached out to rescue me with her kindness and love; and to Pat and Barry Shelton, the best in-laws anyone could ask for.

For their help, support, and funny stories, thanks also to Deborah Hare, Karen Pritzker, Jane Tamarkin, Carolyn Wyman, Joe and Sue Amarante, Fran Fried, Ann Dallas, Mary Colurso, Kim Caldwell, Hayne Bayless, Mara Lavitt, Dave Sigworth, Mary Barton, Ida Massenburg, Kate Flanagan, Tracy Blanford, Edward Mattison, and Alice Elliott Smith. Linda Chase gave me clarity and authenticity.

There's no thank-you big enough for Bruce Bortz, the publisher of Bancroft Press. He read eight years' worth of columns in one week and guided me, humorously, intelligently, and respectfully, through the arduous and baffling process of shaping a book out of them.

For the book, he also asked me to write a bunch of additional columns on work because, he said, I hadn't really focused on the subject in any of my previously published columns. And thanks to Evonne Smitt, who read all the columns, categorized them, edited them, and stayed nice the whole time.

And more thanks than I can ever express to all the people who have taken the time to write and call with love and advice and encouragement and stories.

Sandi Kahn Shelton
Guilford, Connecticut

Contents

My Very Own Poltergeist

Dioramas and Cupcake Recipes

My True Calling

Much More Than I'll Ever Know

Contents

Contents

Social Misunderstandings

A Gender Thing

Nothing More Rewarding

Introduction

Not long ago, I found myself standing in line at the grocery store, when a man in line behind me—a man I'd never seen before—cleared his throat, and said, "So, how did Stephanie's sock bump problem work out?"

"We're turning the socks inside out so the bumps aren't so noticeable," I said.

"Won't work for long," he said, chuckling. "Not with that *Stephanie*. You know how she is!"

A few minutes later, as I was waiting for my check to get approved, the cashier said, "I've been meaning to call the paper and ask them to get a message to you. You know, you should see that your Ben gets a better alarm clock, now that he's in college. There's no excuse for him oversleeping like that last week."

"I'll tell him you said so," I told her. "And your name is—?"

"And, also, I hope you don't mind me saying so, but I liked your picture better when you had the long hair, and you smiled wider. Of course, you probably don't want to smile so wide now because you don't want the camera to show the wrinkles, right?"

I gave her a weak smile.

"Wrinkle cream's in aisle four, if you're interested."

The man behind me said, "Go ahead and get it. I'll hold your place."

Over the years, I've actually gotten used to this kind of

thing. It's what happens when you write a humor column about your family in the local newspaper. People I've never seen before come up and say all sorts of weird things to me.

Once, I was getting out of my car when a jogger paused long enough to critique the haircut I'd written about the week before. (She said that with a forehead like mine, I'd better stick with bangs.) Another time, I wrote a column about buying a hat that exactly matched my purple coat. Afterward, a man stopped me, stared for a minute at my outfit, and then declared, "There's actually a shade more blue in the hat than in the coat, you know."

Over the last decade, my life has pretty much become an open book for the people of South Central Connecticut, where I write for the *New Haven Register*. They've watched my son Ben go from dioramas to dormitories, my daughter Allison grow into young womanhood, and little Stephanie progress from the first signs of pregnancy through birth, toddlerhood, and now to being a regular kid who hates homework.

And they've seen me starting out as a divorced mom of two kids—then meeting a guy, getting married, having a baby—and since then, they've heard about most of the family adventures that followed.

Someone once asked me, "How did you get that man to marry you, when he knew full well that his life was going to be plastered across the newspaper every Sunday?"

Well, it was simple, actually. I promised him I never would write about him.

He, who is also a newspaper reporter, told me right from the beginning that he didn't want to be fodder for my career.

"Fine," I said. "Great. I'll never even mention you."

And I do try not to mention him—really I do—but over the years he's relented. Slightly. The way it now stands is: if it's Tuesday night (the column is due Wednesday at noon), and I don't have a subject yet, *and* I'm crying—well, then, he'll let me tell everybody that he's a Cubs fan. Or that he saves coupons. Or that he had a lousy spatula when I married him.

It's not fair, I know.

It all started innocently enough. I was hired by the paper, you see, to write about a small town outside New Haven. My job was to go to Planning and Zoning Commission meetings and attend school board sessions and write factual, informative stories about the budget and charter revision.

But it was the mid-80s, and somehow I found myself working in a newsroom filled with bright, interesting, intelligent people, all with one curious thing in common: none of them seemed to have heard of children. I was the only one around who had a pair of them, much less *knew* what they were.

People would saunter over to my desk, point to the pictures there of my kids and say, "So what are *those* supposed to be?"

So then I'd find myself explaining about how it was possible for humans to reproduce themselves, and that when it happened, usually you ended up with a small person to live with you for the next 18 to 20 years. I said they were basically a lot of trouble and made terrific messes, but they were cute and said funny things a lot of the time, and that they smelled good when you got them cleaned up.

So, every day, there I'd be, telling everyone all the funny things that had happened in the last 24 hours, when my editor suggested that rather than wasting all my breath talking about this stuff, maybe I could see my way clear to getting some *writing* done, and it wouldn't be such a bad idea to write about these strange small creatures for the newspaper. She'd noticed that other people in our readership also tended to have them, and maybe they'd enjoy my writing on the subject.

The column was born.

A few years later, in 1989 actually, *WorkingMother* magazine started publishing some of the stories, too, and pretty soon people from all over the country were writing me to tell me that *their* kids were screaming about sock bumps too, and that they also couldn't get their toddlers out the door without bribes.

One of those people who happened to run across my *WorkingMother* column was Bruce Bortz, publisher of Bancroft

Press. He called me up one day and asked me to send him every column I'd ever written. I couldn't imagine anyone—even myself—sitting down to read all of them, even the very first one when I didn't know what I was doing.

"That one, too?" I said.

"Yes," he said. (He picked it too; it's the one about taking my father and stepmother along on vacation with us.)

Anyhow, he didn't even flinch when I told him there were 432 columns, and that my kids were all different ages throughout them, and that many of the columns were actually still inside the newspapers and magazines, not even cut out.

"Send 'em!" he said, and so I sent them.

After spending a week reading every word, it was Bruce who finally put into words what I'd been trying to say for 432 columns.

Twenty years with kids can be a long, long time. You might as well laugh while waiting for the next diorama to be due.

Preparation for Parenthood

Forget about the diapers.

If you're pondering whether to have a baby, take it from me: learning to change diapers is the least of it.

Every baby boomer I know who's now wrestling with the question of reproduction has major questions to ask those of us who have seemingly survived having children.

We get asked if it's hard to learn how to work those high-tech disposable diapers, whether spit-up washes out of cashmere sweaters, if breast-feeding hurts, and at what ages babies start sleeping through the night.

My friend Marguerite has just spent a year reading *The First Twelve Months of Life* and *The Magic Years* and all the published editions of *Baby and Child Care* by Dr. Spock. She's sat in on a Lamaze preparation-for-childbirth class, attended a breast-feeding session with LaLeche League moms, and watched a videotape on How to Take Care of a Newborn.

She says she's ready now to throw out her birth control devices and let come what may.

I say she could have better spent the year learning to make an elephant costume in one evening.

She also could have invested her time brushing up on her Pig Latin, so that she and her husband could occasionally enjoy a private conversation in their own home.

And while we're on the subject, I'd like to caution her that before she ends her childless state forever, she should make sure she definitely knows how to cover textbooks with brown paper bags and how to make a recipe of cupcakes come out to exactly 24.

These are the skills she's going to spend her next 10 years using.

Any parent would tell her that, as far as breast-feeding goes, she shouldn't even waste her time researching how many ounces of milk a baby needs. The main thing a new mother needs to know is how to eat spaghetti and nurse *at the same time*. This is a trick that may actually save her life because new babies spend 23 out of every 24 hours at the breast.

Prospective fathers, who now can spend hours pondering whether a plastic bathtub is theoretically better for the tot than the kitchen sink, would do well to instead turn their attention to learning "The Wheels on the Bus Go Round and Round." We child-owners would be happy to supply a copy of the words, with all 50 makeshift verses.

While we're on the subject of songs, it wouldn't hurt future parents to acquire a few dozen lullabies in advance. While some children *will* eventually fall asleep to the strains of "Born to Be Wild" or even your college fight song, most prefer something along the lines of "Toora Loora Loora."

By all means, skip learning "Rock-A-Bye Baby" because many children will listen too closely to the words and conclude you have an accident in mind for them.

These are the things people overlook when they're contemplating giving birth.

If Preparation for Parenthood classes were *really* getting people ready to become mothers and fathers, not only would they be showing people which end of the baby gets the diaper, but they would surely have a session on giving birthday parties for 2-year-olds.

And child birth educators, once they taught women how to breathe to push the baby out, could then explain how to construct a diorama. Those who don't already know that a diorama is a miniature scene depicted in a shoe box, greatly loved by elementary school teachers, might have to take a remedial childbirth course.

There should also be separate seminars to teach such skills as how to put training wheels on bicycles, how to sew patches on jeans, what to do at a PTA meeting, and how to take 24 kindergartners to the local Historical Society.

People who want to know if they're really equipped for parenthood should give themselves the following test: Do I know the difference between Ernie and Bert? Can I read "The Cat in the Hat" five times in a row without outward evidence of mental deterioration? Do I know how to rewind a baby swing without waking up the baby?

And oh yeah. Can I really get that elephant costume ready by morning?

A Team of
Night Watchmen

The Proper Place
to Slumber

Some people know instinctively that the way to get a baby to sleep is to put it in the crib and leave the room.

Those people live in a quieter and simpler universe than the rest of us.

You will never find *them* staggering through the day with black circles under their eyes. They probably can even find their house keys, know what day of the week it is, and remember where their desk is at work. And if you ask them how the baby is, they say "Fine" instead of growling.

As for me, I am writing this column with a 4-week-old baby strapped to the front of me.

And, yes, thank you, she is finally asleep.

The baby and I came up with this system for column-writing because we both now understand that cribs are not the proper place for babies to fall asleep. The baby has let me know that cribs are the places where babies are supposed to wail and thrash around until someone comes to rescue them.

Still, every few days or so, we try out the crib again, just to make sure the rules haven't changed. Who knows? It could suddenly become a habitabe place where a baby could gently relax, close her eyes, and drop off to sleep.

We try it, but according to my friend Jean, we're not doing it with the right amount of Confidence and Perseverance.

You have to just know this is the right thing, Jean insists. You have to believe with every cell in your body that this baby is going to get into this crib and fall soundly asleep. Right now.

I don't have time to indulge in self-hypnotism these days, I tell her, and besides, I know from experience it isn't going to work.

You see, I've already been educated by two previous babies, one of whom would only sleep in a Perego carriage with blue upholstery, moving at a steady speed of 3 miles per hour, and the other who wanted to be held at a precise 47-degree angle and walked back and forth, back and forth, while little-known Woody Guthrie tunes played in the background.

And if ever there were a noise as loud as a flea sneezing three streets away, forget it. Conditions weren't right for sleeping, and the deal was off.

But don't waste your pity on me. Give it to my friend Edward instead. The deal he made with his baby was that he would shake the crib a set number of times and the kid was supposed to fall asleep.

The set number of times was 10,000.

The two of them would stay upstairs for hours and hours, Edward counting out the 10,000 shakes of the crib and the baby apparently waiting for the right number to come up so he could then demand: "More wock."

Or what about all those people with creaky floors? If you are thinking of having a baby, my advice to you is to first tighten up all the floor boards, because just as you have walked or patted or rocked your baby into a tentative sleep, you will surely step on a board that will shout out, "AEEEEEEEEEEEEEEE" and your baby will realize you're making your escape.

Needless to say, babies take a very dim view of escaping parents.

At one desperate point, I actually marked the traitorous floor boards with masking tape so they could be avoided. But other parents I know have opted to perfect the standing broad jump and catapult themselves out of the room and into the safety zone of the hallway.

Many people who can't find it within themselves either to

count to 10,000 or to perform Olympic events opt for the Automotive Sleep Method. This is where you try to bore the baby to sleep by driving around the neighborhood for hours.

The popularity of this method probably explains why there is so much traffic in the middle of the night. But even though it is guaranteed to work, at least until you get back home, you'll eventually resent being forced to drive around every night and you'll most certainly get tired of your friends laughing at you.

It's tough to admit that some 7-pounder has you held hostage in the middle of the night, or that you'll do absolutely anything to get a night's sleep.

But don't let your ego get in the way. The standing broad jump will be a skill you'll have all your life.

Rowing the Night Away

Whenever you happen to wake up in the middle of the night—perhaps to fluff up your pillow or snuggle more deeply underneath your quilt—think of me.

Especially if you glance at your bedside clock and it's between the hours of two a.m. and, say, 4:30, just send a little thought my way. I will be rowing.

Naturally, I don't *want* to be rowing. I'm not even sure I know what rowing is. But there I am, doing things that I hope will pass as rowing, so I can quiet the howling 16-month-old who is demanding that I row.

Night after night we go through the same routine. I awaken to the calls of "Mommy! Mommy!" But then, once I've stumbled to her side, she starts screaming, "Row! Row! Row!"

She doesn't even bother to wake up. There she stands in her crib, eyes tightly closed, hollering at the top of her lungs, in a tone of voice that means she already knows she's going to be disappointed.

She flings herself toward the door. Apparently rowing has something to do with getting out of her bedroom, but I'm too smart for that. Ask anybody. Once you let a kid out of her room in the middle of the night, you might as well forget about getting any sleep again. It'll be orange juice parties, Sesame Street videos, and let's chase-the-kitties-with-the-toy-lawnmower games. All night long. Night after night after night.

So I tell her politely and firmly that we will be remaining upstairs this evening, and that she may have anything on earth her heart desires if she will only please let me go back to sleep.

I have objects on hand that I offer: a bunny that plays "Here Comes Peter Cottontail," a copy of *Goodnight Moon*, a bag of disposable diapers. When these prove inadequate, I look around desperately for others. I would consider unscrewing the handles from her chest of drawers, I tell her, or giving her marking pens, or even the others kids' completed homework assignments. "Row!" she says loudly. And then she starts to scream—pitifully, despairingly.

Next I offer what to any kid is the Key Prize: a trip to Mommy and Daddy's bed.

Pediatricians will tell you this is a big mistake. They put on very concerned, doctorly frowns when they hear of children in the Parental Bed. But one time a pediatrician drew me aside and said, "Sometimes, if you want any sleep, it's the only way. My own children are in my bed at least twice a week."

After that, I realized pediatricians live in the real world with the rest of us, so now I cheerfully tell them everything. "Oh, I offered her the handles from her chest of drawers and three red marking pens, but even that didn't work," I'll say gaily, and I know that underneath that horrified frown lurks true understanding.

So off we go, to the magical land of Mommy and Daddy's bed. But guess what! You can't row in bed. Fool that I am, I am soon discovered not to be rowing, and I am yelled at for it.

"Do you know what row means?" I ask the father of this child.

He has no idea. "Fish eggs? Row, row, row your boat? Cheerios?"

I don't think she knows about fish eggs, and the Cheerios are downstairs, where we are *not* going. I start to sing, "Row, Row, Row Your Boat," but she shrieks.

So I sling her over my shoulder and walk around the room.

Amazingly, she instantly starts to snore—loud, productive, drowsy snores that hang in the air.

"I think I'm rowing," I whisper.

"That's wonderful," my husband says.

Everybody sleeps again, except me. Just when I'm rowed out and plotting to get back to bed, she wakes up screaming.

Rowing has been redefined. It now means I must sit in the rocking chair, upright, clocking 50 rocks per second. She sleeps again.

Twenty minutes after that, rowing means the Bonnie Raitt tape played at half-volume, a bouncing walk around the living room (yes, we went downstairs—so what?), and a cup of orange juice.

Shall I even confess that after that, it means the late, late, late movie, a cookie, and an imaginary conversation on the telephone with Grandma?

"Don't let this worry you," advises the pediatrician the next day. I took the baby to the doctor hoping to hear she has a major ear infection and that once she is on medication, I will never have such a night with her again. But no. There is no ear infection. Instead, the good news is: "This is a perfectly normal stage. Nothing to worry about at all."

I try to hide my delight. I am wondering if I can get my work hours changed to the night shift. Maybe I could even get some sleep.

Patently Absurd

A bad night for my friend Kate is when her 2½-year-old stays up until 9:30.

Sometimes, if I'm feeling very masochistic, I'll even let her talk about how horrible she feels when this happens.

She goes on about how cranky he gets, how cranky *she* gets, how many stories she has to read to him (two), how many songs he needs to have sung (two), and how many times she wishes he would just lay his head down and give up and go to sleep (at least 17).

The whole time I'm listening, however, what I'm really thinking is, "Kate, you're a lucky dog."

She's obviously a woman who doesn't know what a bad bedtime experience can be.

If our 2½-year-old goes to bed by 9:30, one of us is sure to say, "Do you think this is just a nap, or could she possibly be down for the night?"

In fact, we even worry that she might be getting sick if she's not still up doing her famous bath-towel fan-dance when it's 10 or 10:30.

And as for bedtime rituals—well, I'm not trying to outdo Kate in Terrible Children Stories, but a good night at our house is when we get away with reading a mere five stories and singing only six songs.

And shall I mention that the five stories include *War and Peace, Gone with the Wind*, and *Exodus*?

No, no, no. I've gone too far.

It just seems that way. Actually, the stories tend to be along the lines of P. J. Funnybunny's dramatic decision to remain a bunny rabbit after sampling life as a possum, a bear, and a skunk.

Then there's the tale of a clumsy girl named Jackie who discovers gymnastics and becomes "Jumping Jackie."

It's no wonder that a person wouldn't want to nod off when there's so much wonderful reading material in the world.

And then come the songs.

Would you believe "Hickory Dickory Dock," where you have to do all the possible times based on the military clock? And "Wheels on the Bus," where you break the bus down to spark plugs and manifolds, as in, "The manifold on the bus goes whirrr, whirrr, whirrr"?

I know this is wrong.

I know it because parenting magazines trumpet the news every month: "Put Your Children to Bed On Time! They Need Their Sleep and You Need Time!"

Even Dr. T. Berry Brazelton, the child care expert who smiles as toddlers dismantle their homes and take apart younger siblings, gets a deep frown on his face when a parent confesses that little ones might be up—well, past when a parent would like them in bed.

"This is patently absurd," he will say. Those are his exact words: "Patently absurd that a child wouldn't go to bed earlier than this."

And I agree with the man.

But if he could see into my house—and luckily he can't, or he would be saying, "This is patently absurd" quite a few times—he would see that not only is there one little whippersnapper still making the rounds at 10:30 p.m., but the older two kids are still fairly active as well.

In fact, the whole household seems to get an infusion of energy each night along about the time most parents are pretending they don't know any children.

If it's 10 p.m., you can be sure we have several bright-eyed little people running back and forth, suddenly remembering

that their book reports are due tomorrow, searching the refrigerator for snacks that could ease the gnawing hunger they
didn't notice at the dinner table, and generally being alert,
well-informed, and interesting.

This is the time of day they invariably choose to discuss
the world situation.

"Why did the Persian Gulf War start, anyway?" one will
ask.

"Do you think the Cherokee Nation will rise again?"

I used to find these topics irresistible, until I figured out it
was all just a stalling technique.

These days I snarl and say, "To bed!" in a voice T. Berry
would be proud to hear.

It's just too bad it doesn't work all that well. Even when
I've roared, "This is patently absurd!" hardly anybody pays
any attention.

So this is what I want to know from T. Berry and his team
of parenting experts: Is it conceivable that I'm *not* doing too
much wrong, and that this is just what it's like to raise a team
of night watchmen?

There are worse things than that, you know.

And reading about P. J. Funnybunny over and over again
just might be one of them.

An All-Nighter

There is no logical explanation for this, but about once or twice a month, along comes a night when no one in our house gets any sleep.

That is: zero sleep takes place.

In other words, we are *all* awake *all* night long.

No Z's.

Take this night, for instance:

8:30 p.m.: I stood up and declared, loud enough for everyone to hear: "Tonight I am going to get tons of sleep. I am so tired that I could fall asleep right this minute and not wake up until next week.

"Yes sirreee," I went on. "*Sleep* is what is needed here. Good, healing, nourishing sleep."

And off I went with 4-year-old Stephanie to give her a bath, brush her teeth, read her the required two stories, sing the required three songs, and then sit in the dark until a suitable interval passed and she agreed that I could leave the room.

And I actually did make it through the bath, the teeth-brushing, and the stories.

But once we turned out the light, I was a goner. No songs.

9:47 p.m.: I uncrooked my neck, straggled out of her room, took a bath myself, and went downstairs to tell the rest of the family again how wonderful sleep was.

The two older children, both of whom had a day off from school the next day, looked unimpressed. They are teen-agers, which is a time of life when you feel you've already wasted enough time on sleep—unless it's morning.

Allie, who is 13, had a friend sleeping over, and they were still in the stages of mapping out the evening's agenda.

"Go upstairs and go to bed," I said.

11:05 p.m.: I crawled into bed and set the alarm for 7.

"A full eight hours," I said to my husband. "Like normal people."

11:25 p.m.: I went to find out why Allie and her friend were having drill team practice in the guest room upstairs. They insisted they had not actually been marching and didn't have a drum.

"We were piling blankets on the bed so we could be warm up here," Allie said.

"Why don't you sleep in your own room, where it's already warm?"

"It's more fun up here."

"Then use quieter blankets," I said.

12:13 a.m.: My husband got up to investigate the beeping noise coming from 16-year-old Ben's room. Naturally it was the computer modem.

Ben explained that the middle of the night is a great time to talk to people around the country via computer.

His operation was shut down.

1:30 a.m.: Stephanie (Indian name: Elbows So Sharp They Could Kill You) came thundering into our room and climbed into our bed. I grouchily made room for her and her equipment, which included a pumpkin, a teddy bear, and all the books from the Sesame Street Alphabet series.

1:38 a.m.: I suddenly realized that the whispered, "I'm thirsty," every three seconds meant that I would have to go downstairs and get a drink of water for Stephanie.

1:45 a.m.: Stephanie remembered she was owed three songs. We argued about whether we could sing six the next night.

2:20 a.m.: The next door neighbor, whose wife had left that afternoon to have a baby, arrived home from the hospital. The children, none of whom had slept even one wink, all yelled from their beds that they wanted to go outside and ask him whether it was a boy or girl. I shouted, "No!"

3:40 a.m.: Stephanie whispered that she needed to go to the bathroom. I suggested that after that, she might find a suitable place to sleep in her own room. She cried. I said, "Never mind."

4:15 a.m.: My brain finally processed the fact that I was sleeping cheek to cheek with a live, 2-pound pumpkin. I put it on the floor.

5:05 a.m.: Stephanie informed me that the bed was too hot. We rearranged all the covers. I said her room was very cool. She cried. I said, "Never mind."

7:15 a.m.: Stephanie rolled over in her sleep and knocked me with her head, giving me a fat lip.

8:30 a.m.: Leaving all the children sleeping, I went outside and talked to the neighbor, who was walking his dogs. He said his wife had had a baby boy.

"Guess we'll be having some sleepless nights for a while," he said.

I didn't have the heart to tell him that long past the colic and the teething and the 2 a.m. feedings, he'll still have random No Sleep Nights.

He wouldn't believe it anyway.

A Bedtime Story

My friend Jackie has the kind of 5-year-old who tells her he's sleepy at 8:15 every night and who then gets his stuffed bear, kisses everybody, and trots off to bed.

I've actually seen this happen.

All Jackie has to do is say, "Goodnight, honey! See you in the morning!"—and that's *it*. The kid is history until the sun shines.

Some people don't know how lucky they are.

I'm currently in this deal where I have to make up an entire story to get my 5-year-old, Stephanie, tucked in for the night.

And not just a brief run-down about the three little pigs either.

No way.

Somehow we've reached this unfortunate point in our relationship where *I'm* required to come up with plots and subplots and believable characters right out of my head on a moment's notice and Stephanie's allowed to be the literary critic.

As if I *need* a critic at 8:30 at night.

Once, I was in the middle of a very dramatic tale about a chocolate chip cookie who was disappointed because he was the last cookie to be left on the plate after all the others had been devoured.

"No one wanted him," I intoned. "He was worried that no one would choose him before he got rotten, even though he was made of the most delicious flour and sugar and butter and chocolate chips that there are. And . . . "

"This story doesn't really make sense," said Stephanie, out of the darkness.

"Why?" I said.

She got up on one elbow and stared at me, as if I were insane or something. "Why would a cookie *want* somebody to come eat it up? The cookie knows that would be *bad*. The cookie would be gone in someone's stomach if it got eaten up. He doesn't want *that*."

"Oh," I said.

Frankly, I *had* been concerned about the psychological trauma of having the main character get devoured.

But that's just the kind of corner you can paint yourself into when you're making up a story as you go along. You have to figure your way out when you get to the end.

So then I had to have the chocolate chip cookie roll himself off the plate, out the front door and to the corner, where he managed to hop onto a city bus and ride out of town to a chocolate chip cookie farm, where he lived happily with all the other unchosen cookies.

I was just glad the rest of the family couldn't hear.

The next night, I was beginning a story about a little blue jay named Herman, whom I planned to have discover a birdhouse that no other bird had found yet, when she stopped me cold with, "No *bird* stories, please."

"Why not?" I asked.

"Because birds don't have interesting things to say."

"I didn't know that," I said.

Dogs are thought to be as boring as birds and can't be tolerated in story form, unless somebody has a little puppy who's not the main character.

Stories about cats, however, seem to be all right, as long as the cats don't talk like people and wear clothes.

"This is getting too hard," I said. "I don't like telling stories when there are so many rules about it."

"I just want *real* stories," she said. "It's not so hard to tell me things that could really happen."

"Once upon a time, there was a little girl named Stephanie, who was very ferocious about the stories she'd let her mother tell her, even though it was very late and her mother was exhausted and didn't have a single story in her head."

"No!"

"But that's *real*."

"That's not what I mean!"

"Once upon a time, there was a little girl named Stephanie who thought birds and dogs were very boring until one day . . . "

"This is making me crazy," she said.

Making *her* crazy! I felt like somebody trying to get a story in the *New Yorker*.

One night last week, I turned it around and said, "OK, *you* tell *me* a story then. My head is empty."

She said, "Once upon a time, there was a mommy who knew lots of good stories but they got stuck in her head, all except one about a chocolate chip cookie that somehow got on a bus and lived happily every after. I can't think what could happen next. It's too hard to make up a story."

I gave her a standing ovation.

Words of Choice

Learning To Talk

A friend of mine had a baby who didn't speak a word until he was nearly 3 years old, at which point he looked at her one day and said: "I think I'd like to try some Pepsi."

She was so stunned she actually poured him a glass. And then, I presume, the two of them sat down and discussed the situation in Southeast Asia and whether or not the Mets had a chance at the pennant that year.

That's not the way my children learn to talk.

Through the long dry spell of toddlerhood, we struggle together through the nuances of the English language, tossing words back and forth at each other, praying for some understanding. Not much comes.

"Diaper," I say.

The baby says, "Bappoo."

"Stroller," I say.

"Rahroo."

But I can handle this. I can get used to diapers as bappoos, oranges as ahruhs, phones as rows, cookies as gaggies, strollers as rahroos—and yes, after some months of training, I've even accepted the fact that both shoes and juice are goos.

But what gets me every single time—and what I always forget is part of being the mother of a toddler—are those conversations that go like this:

"Mommy."

"Yes?"

"Mommy!"

"What is it?"

"MOMMY!"

"What? What? What?"

"Dee."

I say, "Oh."

But dee is supposed to have meant something to me. I must search for the meaning of dee. The baby waits, expectantly, for my enfeebled mind to grasp what is obviously a very simple concept.

Patiently she repeats her request: "Mommy? Dee." Over and over again.

I go around pointing out possible dees, but I am never correct. I end up explaining that, in the English language, dee tends to be used more as a letter than as an actual word.

"It's one of the preliminaries," I tell the baby. "You know, A, B, C, D. Or it could possibly be used as a prefix, as in delight, debunk, declare. In some dialects, it perhaps could be an article, as in 'de blues.' But never by itself."

The baby is unimpressed. "Dee," she says, even more firmly than before. She knows instinctively that the first rule of teaching language is to be patient and firm at the same time, and to keep repeating what you know to be correct.

But I don't think I should have to learn this stuff. "Instead of trying to convert me to your language, have you ever considered coming over to my side and speaking English?" I say.

You *know* what she says to that.

So I have learned, in spite of myself, a couple of things about dee. I think it's a verb, and from what I can gather, it's a command, meaning: "Stop everything you're now doing and do the opposite!"

If I am pouring her juice in the red cup and she says, "Dee," I know to stop immediately and pour it in the yellow cup instead. Sometimes it means to put my coat back on. Other times I have to stop walking upstairs and head back down.

But mostly, dee means that it's time for another shoe change.

Shoes, you see, are the central fact of babies' existence. I have friends whose babies cry if they're not allowed to sleep in their snow boots.

Fortunately, due to the kindness of friends' hand-me-downs, my baby has lots of shoes to pick from. There are the brown leather boots, the pink puffy boots, the white boots with the tire-like treads, the white baby shoes (to these she says, "Yuck!") and, most thrilling, the black patent leather Mary Janes.

I'll see her staring off in the distance, a dreamy look on her face, murmuring, "Dee," and I know to limber up my fingers for the buckling and tying.

I don't even question it anymore—not even when the request is for the brown leather boot on the right foot and the ever-sexy black patent leather on the left.

But I have a feeling that when she really makes up her mind to speak English, it's not going to be a glass of Pepsi she asks for. The first request will no doubt be for a pair of flaming red leather pumps.

That's something "dee" can never adequately express.

That Word

The first time we heard it, we were sure we were mistaken. No baby of *ours* knew That Word.

But then, a day later, it was unmistakable. Stephanie was flipping though a book of old family photographs, and when she came to a picture of the older children dressed up in monster costumes, she sucked in her breath.

And then it came: "Dame it! I hate this picture!"

Those were her exact words: "Dame it."

Now any parenting expert will be glad to tell you what to do when your 2-year-old swears. You ignore it.

That may not be your first inclination, but that's what you're supposed to do. Keep a perfectly straight face, and go on about your business as though it never happened. Because if you react, these experts warn, the child will know that something is *very special* about that word, and it will become the Word of Choice.

This is not what we did, however.

We, as a group—two parents and two older siblings—rushed into the kitchen, holding our hands over our mouths so she wouldn't see how hard we were laughing. We were *convulsed* with laughter. Tears were running down our faces.

The next day, she fell off her little chair in the living room. "Dame it!" Then there was asparagus for supper. "Dame it!" And then, when it was time for her bath—"Dame it! I don't want a bath!"

We weren't laughing anymore.

And we weren't doing so hot at just ignoring the whole thing either.

My friend Jennifer has a 5-year-old who has been a devoted swearer for quite a few months now. Jennifer dropped the Ignore-It-And-It-Will-Go-Away method some time ago and has taken to sending him to his room.

He reacts with a look of injured innocence whenever he's been nabbed. He has a way of making his eyes go perfectly round just before he says, "What? You mean that's *another* swearword? But I just made that word up!"

She claims not to be amused, but I think this kid has a great future as a psychic. I've suggested that she stop this battle of the wills with him and see that he gets training in reading tea leaves.

Jennifer, on the other hand, doesn't think a simple "dame it" every now and then is worth getting hysterical about.

"She doesn't even say it right; how can you be mad?" she wants to know.

This fits, by the way, with my theory that things other people's children do seem cute and adorable, while the antics of one's own are immediately recognizable as obnoxious.

I tried to describe in graphic terms the precise expression that had come across the face of a well-meaning older lady in the bank when Stephanie realized she wasn't going to be allowed to write out the deposit slip and yelled, "Dame it, I hate this day!" at the top of her extremely well-working lungs.

"That lady knew instantly what 'dame' meant, mispronounced or not," I said. "She *glared* at me."

Jennifer just shrugged. "I don't know what you can do," she said. "I think it's now illegal to wash their mouths out with soap, whatever good that ever did anyhow."

But my friend Rick had the perfect solution. Rick, you must understand, is a perfectly well-mannered person, welcome in almost every public establishment, yet he claims to have had a misspent toddlerhood, turning the air blue with his epithets.

"The answer is manzita," he said.

I had expected something a bit more profound from someone who had been to the edge and back—but no, he assured me, manzita was all I needed.

His parents had him convinced as a child that "manzita" was the most terrible word imaginable. So we've taken his advice and are now having a Manzita Festival at our house—stomping around, carrying on about the manzita milk spilled on the manzita floor, and this is the third manzita time I asked you to put on your manzita pajamas.

Believe it or not, it works.

I knew we had Stephanie convinced when she told me she wasn't going to wear any manzita barrettes in her hair anymore, and that the manzita banana fell off the table.

I have to admit that yelling manzita is a lot of fun.

There's only one thing I'm worried about: What's going to happen when Stephanie realizes that manzita means absolutely nothing, and she's been duped again?

She'll probably be mad, says Rick, but there's not a manzita thing she can do about it.

WKID Talk Radio

I used to think one of life's greatest little pleasures was riding along in the car, listening to songs on the radio.

You know how it is—just you, the road, the music, and the scenery whizzing by. The possibilities are endless: you can tap along on the steering wheel, bounce around in your seat at the red lights, and—the best part—sing as loudly as you like, with only the other drivers to hear you—and who cares what they think of your singing?

All this, however, was in what I've come to think of as the good old days.

These days I'm usually accompanied by a 3-year-old who sees car-riding time as the perfect opportunity to unload a little Personal Philosophy.

There's something so irresistible about Parent-As-Captive-Audience that no car trip is too long, or too short, for a lecture from what I now see is my own personal radio station, WKID, the motto of which would be "all talk, all the time."

We were riding down the road, and the musings came so fast and furious that I ended up having to hunt down a piece of paper and pen while driving, just so I could keep track of them all.

This, mind you, was in one 60-second blitz:

"How come Michael has a chimney when he doesn't even have any children?" (Later I realized this was a veiled reference to Santa Claus.)

"How could babies have hair by the time they're old enough to turn into daddies?"

"Did Daddy have hair when he was a baby?"

"I have a question about mans who fix roofs. How do they get off the roofs?"

"I have another question. Do mans who fix roofs know their phone number?"

"How can houses break?"

"Will our house break?"

"If our house breaks, how will we know the roofer's phone number?"

"Why do people crash cars?"

Fortunately, the one thing about WKID is that, like other radio stations, there's not usually a requirement for listener participation. In other words, the questions fly at me, but I don't have to field them.

But 3-year-olds have more than questions they want to talk about. They also have theories that need to be put out there for parental scrutiny.

A *lot* of theories.

These are just some of the latest I get to think about.

On guests: "I don't believe in guests. I heard on TV that they're imaginary."

"That's ghosts that are imaginary," I said. "Guests are very real."

"I *like* them to be imaginary."

On names: "When I was a baby living in your tummy, did you think about naming me Larissa? I think a baby like me would have been very good if you had named me Larissa. You should have thought about it."

On friendships: "Sometimes you have friends and you just want to fight with them all the time, but the grown-ups say you have to work out your problems, but you don't want to. You just want to fight."

On french fries: "Mommies don't eat them very much, but I eat as many as I can find."

Sometimes, of course, there are other DJs in the car—and, as with any talk show, you can learn a lot. On the way to gymnastics class, I heard a whole program devoted to the Boyfriend Question.

My kid opened the discussion with the inflammatory statement that she has three boyfriends.

"Boys are yucky," answered 3-year-old Laura, a guest on the show. "My brother and I decided no boyfriends and girlfriends because both of them are yucky."

This was an outrage. "Boyfriends are *not* yucky, or I wouldn't have three of them," said my daughter. "You think I want yucky boyfriends? They're nice, and it's fun to talk to them. Want to know who they are?"

"I bet they're yucky."

"It's Sami and Krishna and. . . . and a *pizza*!"

They fell over laughing.

"Sami, Krishna, and an airplane!"

"Sami, Krishna, and a bowl of cereal!"

By this time they were hysterical, barely able even to form words. By the time the true punchline came—"Sami, Krishna, and a diaper!"—WKID had to go off the air.

It was time for gymnastics anyway.

A Law of Parenthood

There are three things new parents need to know that nobody but me will ever tell them:

Spirits that live in the vacuum cleaner can sometimes quiet a colicky baby.

Four-year-olds ask "why?" 437 times a day. (This is documented.)

And parenthood is the most excruciatingly embarrassing job in the world.

There's some hope, though. Colic eventually disappears, and after a while, you get numb to the 149,505 explanations you'll give that fifth year—but trust me on this one: the embarrassment never goes away.

You can plan on it.

Don't even try to fool yourself for a minute by thinking it won't happen to you. Whatever subject embarrasses you most—your weight, the amount of money you make, the loudness of your snoring, the fact that you put ketchup on peanut butter sandwiches—consider it public knowledge.

Sorry, it's the law of parenthood. No exemptions.

Is it bathroom experiences you'd prefer not to discuss in public? Then beware. What happened to my friend Jessica will probably happen to you someday.

She and her husband took their 2-year-old daughter out to eat, an event that right there should win them some sort of medal. Things were going great until Jessica excused herself to go to the ladies' room.

As soon as she was out of sight, Amanda stood on the chair and announced proudly to the other diners: "My mommy has gone to make a big poop!"

The clientele seemed to take this news quite calmly, but when Jessica returned to her seat, everybody in the place burst out laughing at her.

"John, what's going on?" she whispered.

Nice man that he is, he didn't tell her until the next day.

Or there's my friend Ann, whose son recently made his first trip to the men's room with his dad. When he came out, eyes wide, he told the world that his daddy had made a big mistake and peed in the sink.

It took Ann a full startled minute before she realized, "Ah, urinals."

But there were some other shocked onlookers who she's sure weren't convinced.

Perhaps it's sex that you'd like to think of as a personal matter, not for public discussion. Then do yourself a favor: don't have children.

My favorite budding biologist was a 3-year-old charmer at our day care center who greeted people at the door each morning with the question, "Do you have a uterus?"

And there's my friend Jodie's kid who finds it necessary to explain to passersby that his mother is expecting a baby, and just how the baby got into her stomach in the first place.

When Jodie hears him beginning with, "My mommy and daddy love each other very much . . . " she's learned it's time to drag him away.

I also have a soft spot in my heart for little Matthew, a 5-year-old who set the table with his mother's sanitary napkins because guests were there and he wanted "the extra big kind of napkins."

But perhaps the most dangerous kind of kid is the one who's overly interested in other people, who wants to know *everything* about them.

Don't get me wrong: this kid will be a terrific, splendid adult. But it's the meantime you have to worry about.

"Why is that lady so fat?" is a common question my friend Andrea has to deal with, spoken at full volume, of course.

And: "Why is that man's hair falling off his head? Why is that kid on a leash? Why are you putting your hand over my mouth?"

It can make you want to lobby Congress for a minimum age requirement before children can be let out of the house.

But the all-time Most Embarrassing Thing a kid has ever done, at least as far as I know, happened to my friend Sue, after one of those husband-and-wife discussions about how tight money was.

The next day, Sue was stunned to find out from the neighbors that her 5-year-old twins had gone out, door to door, to sell their old potty chair for $5.

And a sweet old lady had actually bought it.

"I'm returning this to you," the lady told Sue later. "I just couldn't say no to such desperate, pathetic little children. But of course, dear, I cleaned it up first."

Five Little Words

Lately, there are five little words that can send me into an attack of hives.

Just five seemingly harmless words, spoken in the piping little voice of my 4-year-old daughter, Stephanie.

"I've been wondering about something."

She always has a frown when she says this—the kind of frown that lets me know a Really Hard Question is coming. It's a question so hard that she has to squint to make room for it in her brain.

"What is it?" I say, and my own brain starts flailing around in my head, dragging out the memory banks, setting up the data bases, getting ready to fire up some extra cylinders if necessary.

But none of that stuff will help me. In fact, nothing I've ever encountered in my past—through years and years of going to school and obsessively reading the backs of cereal boxes and going to lectures and watching PBS and reading books—*nothing*, you must understand, is going to do me even the slightest bit of good when she is wondering about something.

That's because her questions don't ever have to do with concrete things you can explain to somebody who has only been in the world for a limited amount of time.

I brace myself. She looks musingly off into space, frowning.

"I was wondering what those stones are in that park we passed today."

Stones in the park we passed today . . . stones in the park . . . my brain creaks itself into second gear, and, pleased with itself, comes up finally with a nugget of an answer: "Oh! The cemetery we passed in the car. Yes. Well, that's a cemetery."

"What's that?"

So we spend a half-hour discussing death, burials, and headstones. It's a little like being in free fall, hoping something I say finally satisfies her curiosity.

"They put *dead people* in the *ground*?" she asks in horror.

"Yes, they do," I say, hesitating.

"And then they put a stone on the top?"

"Yes." There is a long silence.

"How do the dead people know to go there?"

"They don't go there. They're *put* there."

"I don't think that's a good system," she says.

"It's the best the human race has been able to come up with," I tell her with a sigh.

I can muddle through, somehow, on the questions about death and burials, even the questions about physics and chemistry and how electricity gets in the walls. All that stuff.

But then there are those *other* questions.

Like when she and I were standing in line at Popeye's, waiting to order some chicken, and she spotted a sign that had the word "no" in it, and she had to know what it said.

"It says, 'No Mystery Pieces,' " I said, although if I had been quick enough, I would have said, "No Children's Questions Will Be Answered on the Premises."

"What's a mystery piece?" she asked.

Go ahead. Think about explaining this concept to a 4-year-old. You might begin, as I did, talking about whole chickens and proceeding into chickens being chopped up into parts.

You would be very sorry if this was the way you decided to go.

So then I backed up and launched into the story of dark meat and white meat—legs and breasts and wings—and how sometimes you might get a piece of chicken that wasn't really any of those parts, and that would be a mystery piece. Period. End of story.

"What does mystery mean?"

"It's something you don't know. Like a surprise."

Long, frowning silence. Then: "What do you mean about legs and breasts and wings?"

"Those are parts of the chicken," I said. "When you order chicken, you say which piece you want."

"What if you say mystery pieces?"

"No one says that," I said, a little desperately. "People don't *want* mystery pieces."

"What about kids who like surprises? *They* might want a mystery piece."

"Mystery pieces are bad, bad things," I said, far too loudly. "*No one* would ever want them. They taste yucky."

"Not to me," she said. "Mystery pieces are my favorite kind of chicken."

The Great Imponderables

My friend Phil drives down the road while his two daughters, ages 2½ and 4, call out to him from the back seat:

"Have you ever put a red light on your pizza? Have you ever put a *building* on your pizza? Well, have you ever put a *truck* on your pizza?"

It's a lot of fun. Just ask him.

After a few hours, when they get tired of the pizza topping questions, they switch to pointing to people on the street and asking, "Where is that lady going? Why does that man have a blue car?" Phil's still not sure which game is his favorite.

He's one of those parents who thought he'd survived the Toughest Stage of Parenthood once his kids stopped saying, "Why?" after every statement he'd make. I remember thinking that about my own kids.

You say something like, "We're going to the store."

The kid says, "Why?"

"To buy food."

"Why?"

"Because we have to eat."

"Why?"

"Because we want to live."

"Why?"

"Because life is intrinsically a positive thing, and we want to preserve it."

"Why?"

Once—I forget just how—we made it all the way back to

the creation of the universe in only four "why's." That may be a world record; I'm not sure.

Little did any of us know when we signed up for parenthood that kids' questions never go away. They just get stranger as time goes by.

I hate to tell Phil this, but the question stage coming up in his life is even deadlier than the "why's" or the where-is-that-stranger-going game. It's the dreaded "what-if's":

Child: "What if a big spaceship landed on the roof and spacemen took you with them to Mars? What if the refrigerator had a nose? What if my elbow was an elephant? What if marshmallows were the size of houses? What if I were really a princess on another planet? What if giants came and picked us up and moved us wherever they wanted us? What if food yelled at you when you ate it? What if that flower was really a box of popcorn?"

You: "Oh, my, that would really be something."

Get a recording of yourself saying that, and play it over and over again for the next six months. It'll save a lot of wear and tear on your vocal cords.

I once thought life would be heaven once the "what-if's" were gone. I didn't know that lurking in the next stage was an insatiable thirst for what seemed at first like actual knowledge.

You might think this stage would at least be more interesting. I thought that. I pictured myself reading the encyclopedia with the children and learning why grass is green, who invented the rubberband, and what a camshaft is.

But I am never asked any of those questions. The questions I get asked don't have any answers. When my kids have pondering expressions on their faces, it usually means they're about to come out with something like, "How many sneezes do you think each person gets in a lifetime?"

And when you say, "Well, I'm sure it varies from person to person," they're ready with, "Well, take a guess. What would you say is the average?"

They're known for gazing into space and murmuring, "How many ant footsteps are in one mile?" or "How do we know for sure the furniture stays in one place when we leave the room?"

I suspect that, tough as these questions are, they're pablum compared to what's coming next. I remember my 15-year-old cousin turning one day to his mother and asking casually, "So how docs it feel to know you only have a few decades left to live and you'll never reach all your goals?"

Give me pizza topping questions any day. At least I'm relatively certain I never put a building on my pizza.

Toward the
Front Lines of life

Turning into Teenagers

As the mother of an eighth-grader, one of my main worries is that I soon won't be permitted to wear my purple gypsy skirt in public.

Or my blue gauzy cotton dress. Or that short denim skirt I like so much. In fact, I'm quite concerned that *nothing* in my closet is going to pass the extreme scrutiny of critical teenagers.

"Get ready," warns my friend Susan. "Your hair, your clothing, even the way you stand while you're stirring something on the stove—everything in your lifestyle is about to come under attack."

I break out in a cold sweat when I get such information. How can people live under such conditions? And how in the world can you ever get ready?

I *could*, I suppose, throw out all my clothes and start over, creating a persona for myself that any teen-ager would love to claim for a mother. But deep inside I know this would never work.

I'd just mess up in some other area. Probably the way I put the key in the ignition of the car would turn out to be the stupidest way for anybody ever to do such a thing.

Or maybe my usual way of turning the pages of my book would be really annoying to somebody trying to grow up in my presence.

My own mother, I remember, didn't embarrass me too terribly in the way she dressed. She was actually above reproach, neither dressing too young nor too dowdy for her age. She was always presentable in public, except for one fatal flaw.

She was given to fits of affection that could never be predicted—or dodged. I'd be walking along beside her, and she'd reach over and start *holding my hand*, for God's sake. And she wouldn't let go either, even when I'd make my hand go limp, like some dead thing. I'd always end up having to shake her off, and then she'd get this hurt look on her face and say, "What, are you ashamed to hold hands with your mother anymore?"

I would think it would cheer my kids immeasurably to realize that I know enough not to squeeze them in public.

But Susan says I'll be lucky if I can even get that close to them in public, once they really start turning into teen-agers. A few years ago, she was shocked in a restaurant when her daughter informed her that the condition of her coming along was that she would not sit at the same table with the rest of the family. Instead, she chose a quiet table for one, and never once looked over at her parents.

"You put up with them through all their early years—all the embarrassing things they do, like yelling and throwing food—and then just when they get to the point where you can take them out in public, *they* don't want to sit with *you*," Susan says.

I suppose there is no justice anywhere in parent-kid relations.

Take my poor friend Karen, walking out the door one morning with her daughter, and the kid turns to her and says, "Whatever you do, Mother, don't laugh out loud. People won't know what to think of you!"

Or Ellen, whose daughter tells her every day that she looks like somebody left over from the '60s. Her hair's too straight, her clothes too hippie-ish, her sandals an embarrassment.

"Have you no *pride*?" she asks her mother. "How do you expect me to bring my friends here?"

If the past is any indication, I think I'm in for some rough times. My daughter was only 2 years old when I got the first message. We were munching on some Cheerios together, and she was gazing at me. I was basking in what I took to be toddler-for-mother adoration, when suddenly her eyes narrowed and she spoke her first full sentence:

"Why do you always wear such yucky pants?"

Well, the teen years are upon us and here's the deal I'm willing to make. I'll give up the yucky pants, and I'll even stop laughing out loud in public places. But I'm sticking with the purple gypsy skirt, and I'll put the key in the ignition anyway I damn well please, thank you.

On Christmas Day

They went off with their snorkels, their travel Parcheesi, and a few Babysitters' Club and sci-fi books crammed into their backpacks.

Along with her travel bravado, my daughter was wearing her turquoise Christmas outfit and brand new Reebok sneakers. My son had on the faded, baggy jeans he'd wanted for a long time. Just a few hours before, these had been Christmas presents, still wrapped and under the tree.

But now it was time to go to their other Christmas.

I shouted to them from behind the metal detector: "Don't forget to call me as soon as you get there! And when you change planes in Newark, be sure you don't take your computer disks through the metal detector! And *please*—let the flight attendant help you get your connecting flight!"

I would have liked to add a thousand other instructions: Don't forget to wear your orthodontic rubber bands, don't stay underwater too long when you're snorkeling, look out for each other . . . and call me, call me, CALL ME if you feel homesick or just want to talk.

But you can't say these things in airports, from behind metal detectors. I've learned there are a whole lot of unsaid instructions you just have to swallow and take back home with you.

As it was, they were already rolling their eyes and putting on mock-tragic frowns through their "We're-on-vacation" grins. As seasoned travelers, they especially didn't like the part about letting the flight attendant look after them.

After all, they know their way around airports. Their father has lived in Miami for several years, and they have had a lot of what the divorce papers call Reasonable Visitation with him.

I approve of Reasonable Visitation.

After all, it would be terrible for them to lose contact with a father who loves them—to miss out on a few weeks each year of basking in his affection and catching him up on all their accomplishments.

As part of all this reasonableness, I just have to accept the fact that, twice a year, they spend a few hours alone in the Atlanta Airport, or the Newark Airport, no doubt galloping through terminals to make sure they get the right connection; and that, at ages 14 and 11, they already know more about airport shuttles and baggage claims than I do.

And I have to accept the fact that sometimes Reasonable Visitation comes right in the middle of Christmas Day.

There will no doubt be lots of Christmases when we'll all get up early in the morning, open presents, spend a while admiring new toys and thanking everybody profusely, fix a too-early dinner together—and then head for an airport.

Reasonable Visitation is all so sane and sensible—until you get to the airport gate on a Christmas afternoon.

Then it becomes something else again.

I know there is no easy way for this to happen. A woman I used to work with had a custody arrangement that had her daughter spending one year with her, then the next with her father. Her moments at the airport's metal detector were devastating.

Another friend races back and forth across town each day, because her 3-year-old spends every Monday, Wednesday, Friday and Sunday at her house and every Tuesday, Thursday and Saturday with his father. Her child wears notes pinned to him saying, "Today is Tuesday, so my daddy will pick me up at 3:00."

No easy way indeed.

As my children gathered up their stuff, I searched their faces to see what they were feeling. Did they hate leaving us behind, as well as the mounds of just-opened presents—or were they happily anticipating seeing their father again?

Both, I decided. They waved and jumped up and down and made funny faces at me as they skittered down the ramp. I smiled, too, waved both my arms in the air, and jumped around . . . until the plane was just a little dot in the sky.

I was fine.

But then a woman in a fur coat stepped away from a group of people and touched my arm. She smiled at me and said, "It stinks doesn't it, honey? I know just what you're feeling right now."

"Thank you," I said. And that's when I started to cry.

Mother of a Kid
About-To-Go-To-College

A friend of mine said to my 6-year-old daughter: "So! Are you excited about going into first grade?"

"Well," said Stephanie solemnly, "I would be, except unfortunately we have something very *tragic* happening in our family."

"What?" asked the woman. She gave me an alarmed look.

"My brother is going to college," said Stephanie. "He won't be living with us anymore."

The woman looked shaken. She gave us all hugs and kept patting me on the back with an expression of horrified concern on her face.

Finally I had to just tell her it wasn't all that awful a fate.

"When they get to be 18 years old and have graduated from high school," I told her, "you sort of expect that they might go to college. In fact, this is probably a very good thing, except that now I have to learn to work the VCR."

So far I don't feel any different. Being The Mother Of A Kid About-To-Go-To-College has meant that I get to stand around with him in department stores, saying things like, "Do we really need to buy *this much* toothpaste? Don't you think they'll have toothpaste at college?"

I get to say this about everything: laundry detergent, deodorant, shirts, dental floss, white athletic socks, you name it.

Sometimes I get to say the same old stuff I've been saying to him since he was 8 years old: "I know it's not cold *now*, but in a few weeks you'll thank me for making you buy that sweatshirt!" (He has never once thanked me for making him buy a sweatshirt.)

Then we get to the checkout counter with our cart piled high, and I quietly write a check for $354.94.

That's what it has been like for me.

Until now.

I suddenly realized that not only did I not know how to work the VCR, set the kitchen clock, or make the computer modem send words over the phone lines, I had also never properly warned this child about the dangerous properties of mayonnaise.

"I can't sleep," I said to my husband.

"He doesn't even eat mayonnaise," said my husband. "He doesn't like it. I don't think you have to worry."

"And thank-you notes," I said. "Does he know that after a job interview you should always send a thank-you note?"

"Job interviews are years away," said my husband. "Don't worry."

It was a crazy day. The about-to-depart kid did laundry and packed, and I ran in every hour or so to deliver a news bulletin from the front lines of life.

"Wash your white clothes separately," I said. "And women do not like men who always assume they're paying the check. That's a delicate matter these days. You have to make sure in advance how it's going to be."

He rolled his eyes.

"And that day my fax machine started beeping and you came in and did something to it and it stopped—what did you do?"

"I unplugged it and then plugged it back in again."

I get out the pad of instructions where I've written down the rules for getting electronic devices to work. These are incomprehensible.

For the modem, I must "Type the word 'commo' and then press the F7 key, type in Alt D, and wait for the spade and the house to come up on the screen." I feel as if I've been initiated into some alien culture.

I stand against the doorjamb in his bedroom and watch

while he takes his posters down from the walls, and packs up his computer and desk lamp in boxes.

I am still brave and smiling.

In two days he'll be living with someone else—a guy from Iowa who's assigned to be his roommate—and registering for classes miles and miles away.

I get busy making his favorite dinner and go out to buy raspberries and ice cream for dessert. After dinner we all dance around in the living room, and then he teaches me how to work the Internet, mapping out every little step, and I tell him once again how proud I am of him, and then I remind him that it's not such a crime, you know, to wear raincoats when it's wet outside.

And for some reason, that makes me cry.

The Eye Roll

When she was just a tiny thing, hanging on my every word, I used to say to her: "Come on now, are you always going to be so sweet to me—or is this just some big set-up you're doing so I won't be prepared for the big breakdown later?"

Oh, no. She was always going to be just as sweet.

"And you'll always draw me beautiful pictures and write, 'I LOVE YOU, MOM' on them?"

Oh, yes, yes, yes.

"Are you aware," I said, "that someday you'll turn into an American Teen-ager and be required to think that everything I do, say, and believe is ridiculous and mediocre?"

No way, Jose.

Now fast forward to her arrival at age 14. I am driving her to the airport. I am the same person I was during that much earlier conversation. I tell amusing stories, ask Interested But Non-Prying Questions about her life, and do not even once ask her to get her feet off the dashboard. Finally, I turn on the radio and sing along.

She rolls her eyes and sighs. Loudly.

At first I can't figure it out, but then I realize that *boys* are in the car stopped next to ours at the red light, and she is afraid they may possibly hear me sing. This would be excruciating for the following reasons:

1. I can't sing.

2. What I am *trying* to sing is an ancient Beatles song.

3. *And* I am wearing a purple T-shirt—not a color that befits my status as an Elderly Woman.

Oh, believe me, I know. I was once 14 years old myself, and did enough of those same Eye Rolls to know exactly what they mean. Once, at 14, in a weak moment, I allowed my mother to come to a school function. The woman actually *held my hand* throughout the entire event, and afterward, when we were in a huge crowd, she said in a loud voice how much she *loved* me, for heaven's sake.

That time, I rolled my eyes so hard they nearly backed up into my head and stayed there, but do you think she got the message? No way. She went on to tell everyone in the room just how *proud* she was of me.

To this day, the woman has no idea how she ruined my adolescence.

So I am trying to be a Sensitive Mom. A '90s kind of mom. An I'm-from-the-baby-boom-generation-and-we-invented-rebellion kind of mom.

With this in mind, I politely switched the radio to some rap station whose "music" rattled my teeth—"music" she knew I couldn't possibly sing the lyrics to.

Eye Roll Number Two.

The Crime: Not Acting My Age.

I gave up and turned off the radio. I said, "You know, I'm really going to miss you while you're gone."

"What you mean is that you'll miss all the work I'm always doing for you," she said.

I searched my brain, trying to recall the last time she had done any work for me. Then I remembered. Last Tuesday, when it was a million degrees outside and we were forced to escape to an air-conditioned Burger King for dinner, I asked her to carry the burgers to the table while I got the napkins and straws and coaxed the 5-year-old out of the Burger King Climbing Thing.

Mercifully, soon after we arrived at the airport, they called Allie's plane. She returned my hug by going completely limp until I released her. Then she was off onto the tarmac, brown hair shining, backpack slung over her shoulder, ready to meet the world as an unencumbered person.

I waited until the plane was a mere speck in my view; I'm superstitious about what might happen if I don't stay, squinting upwards, until the very, very last moment.

But then, *freedom*! I ran to my car, turned the radio on LOUD, and sang an Elvis song at the top of my lungs.

Later, I went home and called three friends on the telephone—I *never* get long turns on the phone anymore—fixed myself a glass of iced tea and drank it, alone, in front of the air conditioner. No one came into the room to tell me it was time to drive across town, or to the mall, or to the movies. No one came in to say that six friends wanted to come over and hang out at our house, and could I go rent a video, and would I mind if they walked downtown to buy Chinese food after dark.

I'll have two whole weeks not to hold my stomach in and to wear shorts that she thinks are too baggy. I'll have two whole weeks without even one Eye Roll aimed in my direction.

Believe me, these two whole weeks are not going to be easy.

Thanksgiving Weekend

I never intended to say anything about this, but the fact is that a lot of what people tell you about teen-agers is right on target.

Especially teen-agers, say, who are at home from college for a long weekend.

The thing a teen-ager in this circumstance most resembles is a cyclone, blowing through rapidly on his way to somewhere else, and borrowing anything he encounters in his path: your car keys, most of your cash dollars, and even items of your clothing you neglected to hide.

Believe me, I resisted seeing it this way for a long time.

I did not want to be one of those parents you see whining in the streets about how their kids don't want to spend any time with them. My usual reaction to someone who says such a thing is, "So what? Go get a life for yourself."

But now I have seen.

I have lived through Thanksgiving Weekend of Freshman Year.

We arranged to meet our family freshman, Ben, in New York City, where we would all watch the Macy's Parade together.

For once, he was right there when we arrived at the designated spot. And incredibly, he had managed to lug 150 pounds of his laundry through the New York subway system.

But perhaps most incredibly of all, he managed to get all the *rest* of us to trade off dragging the huge laundry bag as we hailed cabs and traipsed through Grand Central Station in an effort to get back home.

That's how glad we were to see him. When you haven't hung out with your kid for a few months, you'll do practically anything.

For my part, I kept stopping on the streets of New York to make small speeches about How Much We've Missed You and Isn't It Going To Be Great To Spend Some Time Together Again.

Well.

We hadn't been home for five minutes on Thanksgiving night, when he was already four-and-three-quarters minutes into a telephone call to his girlfriend, making plans.

Big plans. *Immediate* plans.

"Could I just take the car and drive to her house? Please, please, please, please?"

"But it's 10:30!" I said. This may rank among the 10 most dense remarks of my entire life. Somewhere in the before-I-had-children recesses in my mind, I dimly remembered that 10:30 P.M. means *early evening* to a teen-ager, that it's a time of night when you are celebrating the fact that you have at least five or six productive hours left before you have to go to sleep again.

I guess I should have known then what would happen for the rest of the weekend.

The next day, after we persuaded him to get out of bed by 2 P.M. by threatening to come into his room with buckets of water, all held by his 6-year-old sister, we told him all the wonderful plans we had made for him: dinner with the family in a restaurant of his choice and then—drum roll here— going out to the movies with family members. Yay! Yay!

He looked genuinely dismayed. He was sooo sorry, but, darn it, this was a night he had arranged to get together with his best friend, who was in town just for that one night, and they had their evening all planned. And, oh by the way, could he get driven to his friend's house, 25 miles away, or should he just borrow the car until morning?

I drove him. Along the way we stopped to buy him a white

shirt for a formal dance he's attending next weekend at his girlfriend's college. He also needed a tie, a new backpack, and a graphing calculator.

The next night he asked if it would be a problem if he borrowed the VCR and perhaps the microwave oven to go visit some other friends, also in town for one night only. They wanted to rent a movie, and wasn't it great that the microwave had a popcorn setting already on it?

But we did get to talk as I drove him back to the train station Sunday night, him and his 150 pounds of laundry.

"Next time you come, it'll be for longer, and we'll really get some time together," I said.

As he got out of the car, he leaned over to give me a kiss. "You know," he said, "I just realized I didn't get a home-cooked meal the whole time I was home."

And folks, I didn't even yell.

A Parade
Missing-Person Plan

There are two kinds of people in the world: Those who would have made a contingency plan with their college-age kid for what to do just in case they *didn't* find each other at the Thanksgiving Day Parade among 2 million other people in New York City—and those who wouldn't have ever dreamed of such a thing.

You'll never guess which category of person I am.

I am the category of person who stands there, stunned, as the parade ends, and billions of people—none of them my own personal son, Ben, a college sophomore—straggle off to get into taxi cabs, trains, subways and cars.

I am the category of person who, once the rest of humanity has gone back to live out their lives, says to the rest of the family and to our friends who came along: "OK, now. How many of you think he would have taken the subway, and how many think he would come in a cab? Who knows what color his new jacket is? And if *you* had missed the parade, what would *you* be more likely to do: go on to Grand Central Station or come to the place where you were supposed to meet your family, in the hopes that they would still be there?"

To myself I am thinking: *How many times in life am I going to be standing in an icy wind trying to second guess what some kid most likely is thinking? And why is it that he was able to get here on time last year when he was a freshman, and now that he's a year older, he can't?*

I am also thinking: Can a person suddenly acquire the

knack for contingency plans, or do you have to be born that way?

It's freezing, so the two younger kids go off to catch a cab, headed for our friends' house in Norwalk, riding with our friends and their new baby. My husband and I decide to stay in New York and look for Ben.

My new plan is to wander the streets until we magically run into him.

"I think he probably is wearing a tan jacket," I say helpfully. This narrows it down to a mere half-million people in New York: brown hair and tan jacket.

"I thought he had a black jacket," says my husband.

"He did, but then he got a new one. It might be tan. I'm not sure."

"It's not below zero, so he's probably not even wearing it," he says.

I find a quarter in the bottom of my purse, and miraculously find a telephone inside a restaurant, and call Ben's dorm room. I leave a pleading message on the answering machine.

When I hang up, I realize I have pleaded for Ben not to have missed the parade, which is not the most helpful thing. I haven't left him the telephone number of our friends' house, where we are all expected for dinner.

After an extended search, I manage to locate another quarter in the other compartment of my purse. This time I leave the phone number on the answering machine and beg him to call.

When we go back outside in the wind, he is still not in the spot where we said we would meet. Street cleaners are by now taking over the world.

We ask each other all the pertinent questions: Might he still be on his way to the parade site, hours late? Is he still in his dorm room, asleep? Would he hear the phone even if he were still in bed? Having missed the parade, would he perhaps call *home* and leave a message on our machine, thinking we would check there to hear from him? Did he start out for the parade and then (pick one): fall asleep on the subway, get the address mixed up, get mugged, meet up with a long-lost friend and start talking about computers, or fall in love with someone and go off to get married before dinner?

We just don't know. So we walk a few blocks, circle back, then glumly decide to take the subway to the train station.

"Eventually," I say, "he'll have to go back to his dorm room—he goes to college there, after all—and then he can call us in Norwalk, and we can come back and get him."

At Grand Central, the 2 million parade-goers have multiplied and become 11 million train-takers. We look at as many of them as possible to see if one of them might be Ben.

We have him paged. No answer.

We are just about to give up and get on the train to Norwalk, when I see him moving through the crowd.

"Hi!" he says. It turns out he slept through the parade, then went to the place we were supposed to meet, getting there 10 minutes after we'd left.

He is cheerful and well-rested. He *knew* he'd run into us at Grand Central, he says. After all, he says, where else would we be?

My Very Own
Pottergeist

The Kitty Olympics

It is the middle of the night.

The house sighs and creaks under the weight of its sleepers. Suspended in dreamlessness, they are lost to the deepest part of the night. Nothing stirs, not even branches or birds' wings in the trees at the window.

There is no stillness quite as still as this.

But at the millisecond of the greatest quiet, when it seems nothing will ever come awake again, what might as well be a shotgun blast rings out through the night.

It's time for the Kitty Olympics!

Tonight's starting signal, brought to us courtesy of an 8-year-old feline named Rhesus, is the sound of a dozen cookbooks being pushed off the kitchen counter onto the tile floor.

That clatter can mean only one thing: the first event will be Toothpaste Cap Hockey.

I wait, tensely, for the clattering of the catfood bowls, the rattling of dishes in the sink, and then the thudding of cats hitting against the kitchen cabinets.

The toothpaste cap is shuttled across the floor, chased by the goalie who bats it with her paws as she goes. There are several suspicious crashes, but these cats are professionals. They know that some crockery may have to be sacrificed during this game. And they're confident we won't ask them to blow their scores by worrying about the protection of pottery.

When the scores have been tallied and the toothpaste cap has gone under the couch, it's time for the Rug Race.

This is everybody's favorite. The cats will even rouse themselves from their mid-afternoon naps just to practice. It's like skiing, stock car racing, and ballet all rolled into one.

They stand, poised, next to the kitchen sink, and then thunder through the house until they meet up with a throw rug. Then they slide magnificently across the floor, doing little twists and turns so the rug gets wadded into a ball by the time it smashes against the far wall. The trick here is for the cat to know just the right moment to leap off before turning into a kitty pancake.

Sometimes the game gets so exciting the cats have to discuss it. There are loud, guttural growls and meows, unearthly noises that can only be imagined in the deep of night.

Hearing their own animal voices freaks them out so much that they launch immediately into the Couch Shredding Championship.

Couch shredding is an event not sanctioned by the human inhabitants. Because it is held in such low regard, the cats squeeze it in between other events so it perhaps will go unnoticed. They are gambling that we will not want to get out of bed for the sole purpose of stopping them.

And they are usually right.

Often following Couch Shredding is the Curtain Climb. This is very daring, not only because it is absolutely forbidden, but because it involves shimmying to the top of the curtain and then leaping off into space and landing on the stereo, a half-room away. Points are taken off for hesitating, and of course, for not landing on the feet.

By the time this is done, the cats are ready for some human contact. They decide to impress us with the Laundry Kill, pulling dirty sweatshirts and jeans out of the laundry baskets and lugging them across the floor to our beds.

We curl ourselves more tightly into sleep as the cats, ears flattened, eyes glowing, proudly fill the bed with the contents of the clothes basket.

By morning, of course, they are soundly sleeping, their Olympic gold medals and trophies hidden away.

We wake up tired and wonder why we put our dirty socks on our pillow before falling asleep.

Snakes

My yoga teacher has decided to retire, and believe me, it didn't take me long to figure out what this was going to mean to my life.

It meant there would be no one around to make me breathe in through my right nostril and out through my left nostril for headclearing purposes, and no one to point out the benefits of standing on my shoulders with my knees wrapped around my ears.

And, let's face it, nobody else I know ever thinks to remind me to open up my *chakras* every day, and then to snap them shut before too much excess negativity floats into them.

Yes sir, I've learned a lot from yoga.

But this really isn't about yoga. This is about snakes.

One day last fall I sauntered over to the yoga teacher and whispered, "You know, I am absolutely petrified of snakes, and I just noticed that I lost my mind for a short spell and bought a house in the woods. So now I need a yoga exercise that will rid the woods of all snakes."

Would you believe that, with all the miracles yoga can accomplish, there still is no exercise that can rid the woods of snakes?

So then I asked for an exercise—hypnosis, lobotomy, *anything*—that would make me mind the snakes less.

She suggested I go rent a National Geographic video and learn about the habits of snakes, e.g., how they don't routinely try to get in people's beds or under their car seats, and how terrific they are for gobbling up all the insects for us.

Obviously she didn't understand that I'm a person who can't look up words in the dictionary that begin with "s" because I would most likely run into a picture of a snake there, and then I would drop the dictionary on my foot in my rush to escape. I would first need a lobotomy just to be able to watch the video, and *then* maybe we could see about the rest of my snake problem.

But luckily, winter came along just then, and since I was fairly certain a snake couldn't pop out from under the four feet of snow that surrounded me, I figured I didn't have to watch a video about how helpful snakes are. Not just then, anyway, when I was already cranky from shoveling out Connecticut every couple of hours.

But now it is snake season once again.

This is a busy season for me because I have to stare at every twig and piece of rubber tire as I'm whizzing along the road to determine if it (a) is a snake, (b) is a former snake, or (c) has the potential for turning into a snake at a later date, which I have always known is a possibility.

It's even worse when I'm relaxing at home. There, I am forced to walk around, peering at holes in the ground to decide if they are the infamous snake holes, or just a place where the badminton net used to go.

Well, I was looking out the window at some flowers I had heroically planted despite reptilian dangers, and there it was:

A SNAKE IN THE FLOWERS.

My former, pre-yoga self would have screamed, "Yeeeeekkkkk!," put the house on the market, and gone to live in a city hotel until the real estate market picked up.

But not me. I am proud to tell you that I watched the snake for some time while I breathed in through my right nostril and then out through my left; I even opened and snapped shut a few chakras; and only then did I rush to find my family members so they could admire how well I was reacting. (After all, what possible good is it to behave well if there is no one around to admire your bravery?)

People were amazed that this was really me. A friend who was visiting offered to kill the snake—and I will tell you this in all honesty: I did not want the snake killed.

Now if the friend had offered to wipe out snakes on this earth, once and for all, I would have had to go for it, any ecological consequences be damned.

But on this spring day, when it was sunny and warm, I had to admit that this one snake did not really deserve to die just for coming near my house.

And OK, so it was only about a foot long and was skinny. A junior snake.

But I knew it was really about yoga. And breathing. And being so brave that my yoga teacher's last words to me won't be, "You really should watch that National Geographic video."

The Puppy

People warned me that getting a new puppy was going to be a lot like having a new baby at home—minus the breast-feeding, of course.

What *no one* dared to tell me is the truth of it: having a new puppy is actually like having your very own poltergeist.

I'm sure the puppy doesn't see it this way.

If he could talk—which thank God he cannot—he would probably report that he owns the place and is getting us into line, and that we are stubbornly attached to some pretty ridiculous things, like the ugly shag carpeting some previous homeowner installed in our family room, which we plan to replace as soon as our youngest child finishes college, or we win the lottery, or both.

This puppy, Sam, wasn't a member of the household for even three days when he clearly determined that this carpeting must *go*, kids out of college or not.

So he set about diligently to remove it, strand by strand. Despite our protests, he would work on this project far into the night, stopping only to pee on it every now and then, in case we weren't getting the idea that this was really vile carpeting.

Call me weird, but I was a little low on gratitude.

When friends would ask me how things were going with puppy training, I said, "Terrific. The carpet we have always hated is slowly disappearing, we're learning to love the gnawed-upon look of our chair legs, and the kids have become so much more physically flexible now, what with trying to eat their meals with their legs wrapped around their ears so their toes won't get bitten."

That's when people started showing up at our house with Dog Training Manuals.

Let me just tell you right now that if you're looking for comic reading, there is hardly anything that can beat a dog training manual.

Take, for instance, what the book calls "the most basic command that every dog can learn"—sitting. (Never mind that I thought the most basic command would be, "Stop nipping at owner for two consecutive seconds.") I am eager to teach this dog something, *anything*, and I would be very proud to have a dog that sits when I think it's a good idea.

The training manual, however, devotes a mere two paragraphs to this lesson, and then assumes you're ready to go on to such advanced lessons as Stay, Down, Heel, and Get Back In The Yard This Instant.

All I can say is that the writer of this book must have been thinking about a different sort of species—both mine and the puppy's. Here are the directions we're supposed to follow:

"Begin with your dog on your left side with his head by your knee in the heel position. Tell him, 'Rover, sit,' and lift up both of your hands at the same time. With your left hand, pull up on the collar while you sweep your right hand up past his nose so he can smell the treat you have in your hand. End up with your right hand above his head. As soon as he sits, praise him: 'Good sit' and give him the treat."

Of *course* we can't do this.

To begin with, we can't even get into the dog-on-the-left-side-of-me position without a major blowout. Then, once the dog realizes I have a treat in my hand, well, you can just forget about this mysterious upward sweep of the hands and the pulling-up-on-the-collar business.

As a novice dog owner, I have to report that my puppy now thinks the word "sit" means Jump Wildly in Midair and Take Part of Owner's Hand Off.

Another amusing entry was under the Housebreaking section.

"Until your dog is housebroken," the book said ominously, "you must tether him to you."

I ask you: Is there a soul in America today who would willingly tether herself to a 12-week-old puppy who thinks that shag carpeting and table legs look like gourmet snacks, and who intentionally refuses to learn the simplest command a dog could ever be taught?

The answer is no.

I think these Dog Training Manuals may be beyond us. There has to be something simpler we can do for assistance.

Maybe we could tire him out by letting him gnaw on his training manual for a while.

A Rustic Retreat

The advertisement in the paper had made it sound so lovely.

"Rustic, shady cottages on the banks of Lake Champlain, in Shoreham, Vermont, rowboats, swimming, fireplaces, screened porches."

It had been back in April, when the word "swimming" had almost a magical connotation, that we sent off the check. Upon arrival, though, on the hottest night in July, it occurred to us we should have perhaps paid closer attention to the word "rustic."

"Because surely," said my father, slapping himself on both arms and his face all at the same time, "that meant mosquitoes. And God knows what else."

The landlord, a drawling Yankee farmer with a glistening bald head, explained exactly what else it meant: the water coming out of the tap was lake water, good only for showers; the water in the well was sulfur water, OK for cooking if you boiled it first; and, oh yes, there had been a big storm and the power was out.

"But here are some candles to use while you get situated," he said. "Hope you enjoy your two weeks!"

One child was sick from all the peanuts he'd eaten in the car. The little one, exhausted, had burst into tears. The rest of us couldn't seem to stop leaping at the walls, swatting at the swarms of mosquitoes.

It was a night of muffled sobs, the slapping of flesh, muttered curses, and every now and then a true howl of distress from one or another of us. I pulled the sheet up over my head, trying to shut out the high-pitched whine of mosquitoes; but then, sweltering, kicked it off again and surrendered to being bitten.

Around 4 a.m. we learned the true meaning of desperation. At that hour, the mind was gone, and a new reality took over. Events were out of focus and somewhat lurid.

That's why, when I heard the laughter starting up, I initially didn't think anything of it. At first there was a chuckle. Two chuckles. Chortling. Then loud guffaws. My parents were hysterical, and soon the children joined in.

This was not normal laughter, understand. This was the stuff you would expect to hear in the dungeons of insane asylums in the 1800s. I had to get up to investigate. I armed myself with a rolled-up newspaper in case they were dangerous.

I peeked around the corner. The first glance was not reassuring. The four of them had lamp shades on their heads—little crowns, which they explained to me through their tears of laughter, were going to be the solution to the whole vacation problem.

"When you have this lamp shade on," said my stepmother, normally a very sane woman, "you can make a tent to sleep under. Mosquitoes can't get to you."

Then, seeing the look on my face, they collapsed in hysteria all over again. But within another 10 minutes, everybody had fallen asleep, all underneath sheet tents held in place by lamp shades.

The landlord came back in the morning—foolish man!— to see how we'd fared during the night. We didn't kill him on sight, as we had plotted.

Instead, we showed him the welts dotting our arms, legs, and faces. We outlined for him the paths the mosquitoes had taken as they buzzed around our head.

He listened, puzzled. "Funny thing," he said. "Nobody's ever complained about mosquitoes here before. I guess it's just because you let them in the house when you arrived. Shouldn't leave the door open, you know."

He walked away, already having pegged us as troublesome city-dwellers who would make a fuss about everything.

After he left, I looked around the cottage. The lamp shades were still on the beds.

I knew we'd stay.

Splitting Hairs

I'm afraid I have noticed an alarming development at our house. The dog is trying to talk.

He is not at all interested in remaining The Creature in the Household Who Barks, which, I have explained to him again and again, is the only role he is suited for. Oh, I've done all the right things to raise his self-esteem about this: I've assured him that forever and ever he will be the only one in the house who is permitted to bark, and that, in fact, that's why we hired him as the family dog in the first place, so he would bark and maybe protect us.

I even told him that we *respect* him for his bark.

You know what he says to this?

"*Oowww . . .*"

This, as our 7-year-old daughter, Stephanie, explains, means that he wants to go out.

She feels qualified to interpret his speech because it wasn't so long ago that she, too, was struggling to make herself understood by using as many noises as she could string together.

I have to admit that, whenever he says this, he does want to go out, because he will look right at the nearest person, say "Oowww," and then rush to the front door, wagging his whole body while he waits for that person to get the idea.

This is fine with me. I actually find it kind of touching that a dog would work so hard to learn English. After all, the dog has already learned that pooping in the family room is no longer an OK thing.

That's not what is so alarming.

The thing that really bothers me is that now he wants to talk at other times—and not just barking either.

He'll be in the kitchen, for instance, idly barking away in a conversational tone of voice, and I'll go over to him, just as his trainer instructed me, and I'll say, "QUI-ET!!"

I say this as ferociously as I can, in such a no-nonsense tone that my children actually turn pale.

He barks again.

This time I yell, "QUI-ETTT!!!!" with additional exclamation points, and I put on a face for his benefit that would re-freeze melted ice cream.

This time he does not bark back at me.

He talks.

He looks right at me and then forms his mouth into awkward, yawn-like shapes, and he—well, he makes a speech. There's no other word for it. He sounds like a phonograph record that was designed for 78 rpm being played at 33 rpm instead, and the look on his face is so intent and earnest that you just know he thinks he is really getting his message across.

And in fact, he is. I know exactly what he is doing: he is arguing.

He is saying, "Look, you people are talking around here all the time and whenever I try to bring up some subjects that I think are interesting, you tell me to be quiet. And while we're on the subject, why is it that you humans get all the potato chips and I have to stick with Puppy Chow day after day?"

He and I both know that he is not doing anything that would fall into the "Dog, Barking," classification, so that he should not get yelled at again.

Believe me, anyone who has kids already is wise to this tactic. *Splitting hairs*, I believe, is the technical term.

I see this in other areas with him also. After many hours of training with a Certified Canine Trainer (much to the amusement of our friends, who believe, I think, that *anyone* should be able to train a dog without professional help), we have taught this mongrel the glorious concept called Down Stay.

I love the Down Stay, and at first the dog did, too. He was very proud of himself for his sterling obedience in this matter. But now when I put him in the Down Stay, he does what can only be classified as the Down Snake, where he scoots along on his belly across the room and goes wherever he pleases. I have even seen him snake his way over to the potato chip bag.

If you yell at him for this—and how can you not?—he gives you a look like, "*Sheesh!* A puppy can't do *anything* around here!"

I say to him, "That's right. If you're going to be a member of the family, you have to behave yourself."

I'm half-expecting him one day to look at me and say, "Chips! Right now!" That's what he's practicing to say. The only obstacle is making that "ch" sound.

Dioramas And Cupcake Recipes

Baby Technology

People are always asking me if I think it was a good idea to have children, and if so, do I recommend that they have any.

I don't know why they pick me to ask.

Perhaps it's because I usually have dark circles under my eyes, and I walk stooped-over, as though I am permanently pushing a stroller. Childless people can't believe any thinking person would willingly put herself into this state.

Take my friend Diana for instance. She and her husband, Barry, have been married for three years now and talk a lot about having kids, but somehow they never come up with any.

"I really want a baby to hold and play with," she told me the other day. "But there's something scaring me away."

I was all ready to reassure her that childbirth and night feedings aren't so bad. But then she whispered, "It's the paraphernalia."

She handed me a catalog. I must admit that I'd never seen anything like it before. It was completely filled with infants' devices—a contraption for every moment imaginable. Until then, I had thought the outer limit of baby technology was reached when they invented those little plugs you stick in the electric outlets when they're not in use.

"I'm just not intelligent enough to raise a child today," Diana said. "What if I went out one morning and forgot to plug in the Wiper Warmers? I would feel just terrible if the little bunny had to have his bottom wiped with a cold cloth."

And then there's the matter of the Lac-Tote. That's a tiny portable refrigerator where nursing mothers can store their milk when the baby's not around.

"I'm sorry," said Diana. "I don't have room in my handbag for a three pound refrigerator. And even worse, I think I'm too selfish to make room."

She flipped the pages. "And what about this video scanner for the baby's room?" she said. "Don't tell me I can get along without that. Or this teddy bear that plays a Brahms lullaby for 15 minutes while the light gradually dims, and then starts to play again if the baby cries in the night."

As I looked through the catalog, I could see what she meant. Almost immediately I spotted the thing I can't live another day without: a plastic holder for juice boxes that keeps babies from squirting apple juice all over.

"Where's the order form?" I said. "I must have this!"

You've got to hand it to the baby boomers. Infants were spared technology until the boomers discovered parenthood. Now it's hard to believe people ever got by without pacifiers that display the baby's temperature, special bathing hats that keep shampoo out of a baby's eyes, and cuff holders to keep babies from tripping on their baggy blanket sleepers.

How did we take trips without a diaper bag that converts into a crib, or a high chair that doubles as a potty seat? Can we have gone in the car thousands of times without the special umbrella for the car seat to protect the baby from the sun?

No problem is left unmanaged. There are devices that automatically cause the crib to rock when the baby makes a noise. And a vinyl pad to put over the edge of the tub so the baby doesn't have to touch the cold surface. Special knitted knee protectors for babies to wear over their pants while they crawl. Metal clips to keep their shirts tucked in.

"How do people remember all this stuff?" Diana wailed. "What if you forget the pacifier that serenades the baby to sleep? It's not like you can just pop into any drugstore and pick up a new one."

"Babies got along for centuries without all this," I said

weakly, but I could see it didn't matter to her. Once you know that you can purchase a special gum-brush to get babies used to dental hygiene, how can you do without one?

"I can't believe you didn't have the special sling for cuddling the baby, or even the nursing tunic so people can't tell you're breast-feeding in public," she said.

It's true, though. Nor did we have the learning center for the car, the special air purifier for the nursery, or the Stroll n' Sip bottle to attach to the side of the stroller.

I like to think of myself as a pioneer. My first baby was born back when we had to rock the crib by hand.

A Hat for the Baby

I made up my mind that I wouldn't take the baby for even one more walk in the stroller until I had my sign made.

The sign was going to say:

THIS BABY DOES NOT NEED A HAT.

"Oh, come now," said my sister. "Let's go for a walk. Why do you need a sign about the baby's hat anyway?"

"Watch this," I told her. I walked outside with the baby. Within 30 seconds, a car had slowed down in front of the house, and a woman poked her head out.

"Shouldn't that baby be wearing a hat? It's only March, you know!" she called.

If I had had my sign made, I pointed out to my sister, I could have just held it up. The Baby Hat Vigilante would have just ridden by without bothering us.

"Wouldn't it just be easier to put a hat on the baby?" my sister wanted to know. She is ordinarily an intelligent woman, but she doesn't have any children, so she doesn't know about these things. For all she knows, when people stop to talk to mothers with babies, they are saying things like, "What nice blue eyes the baby has!"

"I'll show you," I said. I put the baby's hat on her. It didn't take long for a woman to stop us and peer into the stroller.

"This baby is far too hot," she said sternly. "Can't you see the sun is out and the heat is making the baby sweaty? That's why he looks so sleepy."

"Thank you very much," I said, "and by the way, this is a girl baby."

"No," the woman said. "I can tell it's a boy baby because he's dressed in blue."

"Girls don't always wear pink, you know," I said. "This happens to be a girl. Really. Believe me."

The woman smiled. "I can always tell," she said. "It's a boy."

My sister was ready to step in, already angry. I touched her arm and smiled. "It's no use arguing with this lady," I said. "She sees right through us."

It was a nice day, and so we kept walking. Soon the baby started fussing, and a man hurried out of a doorway to advise feeding her.

"She just ate before we left home," I said. "She's actually just a little bit tired, but she'll fall asleep soon."

"You young mothers," he said, "don't realize that you need to always have food along for a baby. You think babies just need to eat on *your* schedule."

I whipped out my personal cookie stash from my purse. He nodded in approval as I gave the baby a cookie.

But further down the block, a woman grew hysterical at the sight. "Don't feed the baby cookies when she's in a stroller! Don't you know that, if you go over a bump, the baby will choke and die? And if that doesn't happen, she could lose an eye with the sharp end of that cookie!"

"I really think the baby will be OK," I said gently.

The woman glared. "Obviously this baby should be home taking a nap instead of being lugged all over town, and without even a blanket yet! It's no wonder her nose is running."

Two women walked by and shook their heads sorrowfully. "I thought anyone would know babies are happier in backpacks," said one to the other.

"Why do all these people say such horrible things?" asked my sister when the women had gone.

"It's their responsibility," I told her. "Because they've had children themselves, they want to make sure the new generation grows up happy and healthy."

But I was at the end of my patience.

We stopped at the art store for a large piece of poster paper. The sign I'm going to make will say:

THIS GIRL BABY DOES NOT NEED A HAT, IS NOT HUNGRY, WON'T DIE FROM EATING A COOKIE, AND HATES TO RIDE IN A BACKPACK.

I'm just hoping we can get that and the baby in the stroller.

Gymnastics for Tots

Let me say at the outset that I was the kind of kid who was once asked to resign from tap and ballet classes.

I was wasting their time, they said. I was uncoordinated and unmusical, and I had no rhythm. And that, the teacher implied to my mother, was sugarcoating it. Push her any further, and she'd say what she *really* thought about my dancing ability.

"For three weeks, we've been trying to teach her the shuffle step, and she *refuses* to learn it," the teacher said, glaring in my direction.

Thirty years later, I'm still practicing that shuffle step—quietly, of course, and off by myself—and as soon as I get to the point I can do three in a row, I'm going back to show that dance teacher how wrong she was.

Just about the time I was emotionally healed from tap and ballet classes, along came modern dance in high school.

I flitted around the gym with the rest of them, dipping and leaping to the best of my ability—but it was no good. The teacher pegged me as a rotter right from the start.

She gave me a D-minus, told me it was a mercy grade, and asked me never to mention to anyone that she had once been my teacher.

Is it any wonder I was forced to take to the typewriter at a young age?

This also explains why, on Saturday mornings, I sit in the

parents' section of a gymnastics school and watch my 2-year-old daughter doing unimaginable things at the top of a ladder.

After all, parenthood gives one a chance to correct those little deficiencies in life, right? You get to relive the past and make it turn out more glorious this time around.

Still, it's probable that no one in her right mind would sign a toddler up for trampoline-jumping. If you took a survey of the mothers in the parents' section, I'll bet we'd all turn out to have been branded uncoordinated klutzes back in our younger days.

I have to admit that I didn't think through this gymnastics-for-tots idea clearly enough.

I thought it would be kind of cute, you know, to see a chubby little former-baby toddling about in leotards and tights and doing toe-touches on the cushions.

I forgot that these classes were going to be taught by people who are Certified Gymnasts, and who think nothing of doing triple back flips in mid-air while eating tuna fish sandwiches. They even do one-handed cartwheels just to get to their cars in the parking lot!

But it now seems I have turned my delicate little baby over to the kind of people who don't innately understand that human beings weren't meant to walk on high beams while playing a game called swivel hips.

"She's doing great," the teacher said to me after the first class—a class I had spent whimpering and peering through my fingers to see what ropes my daughter was now dangling from.

"Did I perhaps forget to mention that she's 2 years old?" I asked in my most polite voice.

I always use this voice when I'm talking to Authoritative Experts, who no doubt have plenty of on-paper support for the kinds of notions they entertain, but who may not realize that real live kids are not all the same.

"She's not even that great at climbing stairs," I said nervously. "I mean, we sometimes have to hold her hand. And we *never* let her swing on ropes or walk along the back of the couch."

The teacher looked unconcerned. "We stay right with her

at all times," she said, "and she's quite coordinated actually. She knows what she's doing."

My daughter, meanwhile, was charging off to the trampoline, where she pulled herself up and began to leap three miles into the air with each jump.

I wanted to run out and warn her about the slippery surface, the sharp springs, the fact that she might hit her head on passing aircraft, and a few other medical facts she might need to know—such as what oxygen deficiency can do to brain cells.

But I held tight.

And I only whined softly when she walked backward on the balance beam, and then stopped to lean over and pull up her sock. By the time she straightened up and gave me a proud wave, I could actually manage a weak smile in her direction.

That's what you have to do, you know, if you don't want children's gym teachers to make fun of you.

Parental Conversationese

I was startled to overhear a woman talking about my child. She poked her friend in the ribs and whispered, "Look at that baby behind us. Have you ever seen a baby so . . . focused?"

I looked down at little Stephanie, sitting calmly in her stroller, feeding a banana to her plastic doll. First she cooed at the doll and tried to coax it into biting the banana. Then she started growling while she mashed the banana into the doll's face.

Focused indeed.

I knew I was in the company of a fellow mother. Only another parent would come up with a good word like "focused" when what she meant was what I say about Stephanie to my husband nearly every day: "This is the most stubborn baby I have ever seen!"

Parents are like that, just by instinct. Before you've even gotten home from the hospital, you're already speaking Parental Conversationese, an intricate mesh of code words and euphemisms, designed specifically for parents who are discussing each other's children.

You get your first crack at using your new language when the nurse brings in your hospital roommate's squalling, red-faced new-born—a kid whose shrieks have already caused several bus collisions in the street four floors below. Automatically you find yourself saying, "Wow, he's got a great set of lungs on him, doesn't he? Nice to see such a healthy kid!"

Well, what else can you say? "Living with that child is

going to be hell for the next 20 years" comes to mind, but has a sour taste to it. Besides, your roommate would probably turn and mention something about how your baby's head has a funny point to it and that you'll have to spend millions in plastic surgery to fix it.

What's funny is how automatic this new language is. One day, it seems, you're a childless person not afraid to call a brat a brat, and the next day you find yourself at the park, watching innocent babies being terrorized by a 3-year-old psycho killer, and you're saying mildly: "My, your little Sam is a real go-getter, isn't he?"

I actually once heard myself telling a friend of mine that her daughter Melissa was very "artistic, in an independent sort of way." This was Parental Conversationese for: "While you were gone, Melissa wrote all over our walls with a green crayon."

Why get specific? When somebody else's kid is really driving you crazy, it always works to say, "Jeffrey really seems to be having a hard time this morning, but I'm sure it's just one of those phases. They all go through them, you know."

An alert parent will know you think she should immediately call in the child psychiatrists to figure out why her kid insists on barking while he eats.

School teachers and day-care providers have to become masters of this kind of language, whether they have children of their own or not. When a nursery school teacher tells you that "little Michael had a very active morning," she probably means that Michael broke the arms and legs off all the baby dolls, smashed the Sesame Street records, and pulled the fire alarm.

And when she says your child is certainly a free spirit, try not to beam too broadly. This is code for, "She won't agree on anything the other children want to do, and insisted on not wearing a coat, even when it was 20 degrees outside."

When you're keeping somebody else's kid—a brat who gets into your cosmetics and paints the faces of the other children while you're on a 10 second telephone call—you'll be shocked to hear yourself explaining the incident to the mother. The words "brat" or "cosmetics" will never be uttered. You'll say, "Joyce certainly has a flair for fashion."

And what do you say when little Lucy climbs up on the kitchen cabinets and you have to call the fire department to have her rescued? That comes out as "My, she's well-coordinated for her age."

I know speaking like this may seem to have its drawbacks, but it's actually quite a useful system. It makes it possible for parents to talk to each other in the playground, even while their own perfect little child is trying to learn to get along with the free spirits and the active, well-coordinated fashion experts around her.

After all, it can be very lonely being the parent of the only wonderful kid around.

The "B" List

It's time I faced facts here: I seem to have fallen out of favor with my 4-year-old daughter.

My first inkling of this came when my husband and I got home from seeing a movie, and there was the usual note from Stephanie on the table.

I have always treasured these notes. Whenever we go out, she forces whoever is baby-sitting to take dictation while she expounds upon her great love for us and tells us just how much she missed us. Then she draws hearts and teddy bears all over the page.

This one said: "Dear Mommy and Daddy, I missed you when you didn't put me to bed tonight. Daddy, will you come in and give me 71 hugs and 341 kisses? Mommy, I would like you to give me two kisses and zero hugs. Love Stephanie."

Then there were the obligatory hearts and bears, and on the back, it said, "Daddy, these hearts are for you. Mommy can have the bears if you don't want them."

I know when I'm on the outs, believe me.

But, as if I needed any more proof, the next day I poured her apple juice, and everything about it turned out wrong. I selected the most despicable Tom and Jerry jelly glass in the world. And then I didn't fill the glass high enough, and besides all *that*, she didn't even want any apple juice.

"It *was* what you asked for," I pointed out.

"Well, I didn't expect you to pour it right now. I'm not in the mood for apple juice right this minute."

"Then why did you ask for it now?"

The hands went on the hips. "Because I didn't think you would pour it now anyway!"

A few minutes later, I overheard her asking her older sister for some apple juice. "*She* doesn't know how to do it right," she whispered. (It's a law of parenthood that you're in trouble when your kids start calling you *she*.) "She even put it in the Tom and Jerry glass with the kite on it. I don't know why she would do a thing like that to me."

Later I tried to remind her that the Tom and Jerry kite glass had once been her very favorite. Sort of like *me*. She gave me a pitying look.

My star has never really risen since. When she gets tangled up in covers in the middle of the night, Daddy gets the call. If a baby doll needs a Band-Aid, she gets it herself. Sometimes, if she's desperate, I *might* be considered a passable partner for a game of Fish or Mickey Mouse Yahtzee, but this is only when nobody better is around.

Let me tell you, this has been a long tumble from my lofty position as the Favorite Person in the World.

From the time she was brand new, those little baby eyes would follow me wherever I went. And then as soon as she could walk and talk, she'd put her pudgy little hands on my face and tell me again and again how much she loved me. Sometimes she'd have to wake up in the middle of the night and come to find me just because all her adoration hadn't been expressed during the day.

And now, here we are a few short years later, and she's saying things to me like, "Why isn't your hair long and black like Patty's hair?" "Why don't you ever make strawberry cakes?" "Did you know your boots look yucky on you?" "Oh, tell Daddy I'm ready for my story and my goodnight kiss."

I'd probably be taking this really hard if I hadn't been in this spot before. After all, my two older children showed me long ago that my place in the sun isn't really a permanent seat, just a loan.

And I have to admit something: There are quite a few unexpected side benefits to being Currently Out Of Favor.

Take those calls in the middle of the night. Guess who now stretches, sighs, rolls over, and goes back to sleep? I'm also the one at the dinner table who gets to eat all her own food without any kid climbing in her lap, begging for seconds, needing everything cut up and then cut up a different way.

And at story time before bed, I can only be trusted with the one-word-to-a-page books. *Daddy* gets the tomes about Barbie losing her friend's wedding dress. I smile at him. He looks pained.

I know it's temporary. He's bound to reach for the wrong glass, wear some yucky clothing, or cut up the meat the wrong way. And I'll be back in favor, my little vacation over.

I just hope I'm ready when it happens.

Sock Bumps

I could almost tolerate the idea that summer is over and we have to put up with cold weather again, if it weren't for sock bumps.

Don't bother asking me what sock bumps are. I have personally never had this agony with my own socks. But as soon as it gets too cold for children to wear sandals anymore, I hear about sock bumps nonstop.

And let me tell you: sock bumps are *excruciating*.

I know this because I get the Every Half Hour Sock Bump Update, delivered by my 5-year-old daughter, Stephanie, at a voice pitch that can cause the wall-paper to peel right off the walls, cereal bowls to shatter in the cabinets, and trees to topple in the front yard.

It starts with, "Moommmm, I have a sock buuuuuuuummmmmp." (Didn't I warn you about the voice pitch?)

Here are the three things I've learned that you must never say in such situations:

1. "What in the world *are* sock bumps, anyhow?"

2. "Just wiggle your toes and the sock bump will go away."

3. "Congratulations! Only very special wonderful people get sock bumps. Just tell yourself how lucky you are."

No. What you must do during a Sock Bump Attack is go over to the stricken child, remove the shoe, and stare for a very long time at the sock.

You will not see anything, of course. Just a foot inside a sock. But if you're smart, you will frown, pull at a couple of the toes, and growl as you tug at the sock. Then put the shoe back on, sign, and announce that this sock bump was caught just in time.

Say in a very loud, confident voice: "There will be no more trouble from sock bumps, I can guarantee you that."

Naturally, five minutes later, you'll have to do all this again.

This time you will have to be more ferocious with the sock bump. You will have to threaten it with some kind of harm (perhaps unraveling) if it fails to disappear this time. Rattle the toes around. Thump on the bottom of the foot for good measure.

Then hold your breath and try to get very busy with something that preferably requires you to leave the house.

I am a veteran of the Wars Against Sock Bumps, but I have to admit that even after years of combat, I have never managed to rid the world of sock bumps for more than 20 minutes at one time. It's a little like the war on drugs.

No wonder I dread autumn.

This is the time of year when my efficiency drops to near zero. At night, when I'm ticking off what I've managed to accomplish during the day, all I can really point to is that I have glared at Stephanie's socks a total of 50,000 times and have said many insulting things to the seams of her socks.

But the score always remains at Sock Bumps: 4 million. Me: 0.

"We're going to get to the bottom of this problem," I told her. "We are being done in by pieces of cloth, and we have to fight back."

"I don't think you can fight with sock bumps," she said. "They're sneaky and they know how to move around in your shoe."

"We will buy new, improved socks, then," I said. "We will spare no expense."

So we went shopping for socks—and I'm not talking about the ones you can buy in packages of 10 for $3, either. We went for the high-priced line—the kind that have received special blessings from clothing manufacturers and have had their little bump demons exorcized. Heck, I even shelled out for the ones with lace around the edges and appliqued animals near the ankles.

If you are currently at war with sock bumps in your own life, take my advice—money can't help you.

These fancy socks behaved themselves OK in the store, but once we got them home, they turned out to have many sock bump gremlins lurking in their high-priced threads.

"Well, kid," I said. "Would you like to scrap the idea of socks altogether and wear tights every day?"·

She wailed loud and long.

Apparently sock bumps are *nothing* compared to what kind of evil spirits live in tights.

"Tights try to *kill* your feet, but socks just want to make your feet crazy" was the distinction she made for me.

"Oh," I said.

But what I wanted to say was: Just wait, kid. Wait until you have to put on pantyhose every morning. *Then* we'll talk about sock bumps.

An Enlightened Parent

In one week, I said three things I swore I'd never say to my children.

I said: "Get down off there right this minute, or you're going to fall and break your neck and never walk again."

I said: "What can you possibly have to say on the telephone for two hours when you've been with your friends all day in school?"

I said: "You shouldn't be listening to that kind of music. Do you even *know* what those lyrics mean?"

So much for being an Enlightened Parent.

Twelve years of reading how-to-parent books have just gone down the drain. You won't find a single book on kid-rearing that will ever advise you to mention broken necks as a way of keeping a toddler from standing on the dining room table. I know. I've read them all.

I've read books on how to talk so kids will listen, and how to listen so kids will talk; how to raise stress-proof, crime-proof, drug-proof, failure-proof children; how to keep children from growing up too fast or staying little too long; how to win fights with them without ever raising your voice; and how to parent them effectively every moment of the day, without ever losing the smile off your face.

Oh, I have been well-trained in the lingo, believe me. Back in the late '70s, I wouldn't have ever blurted out anything as spontaneous as the three things I said this week.

I would have consulted my Pocket Guide to Parenting and said something like:

"Oh, my goodness, you must be feeling very adventurous to want to walk around on the dining room table today! Why don't we use the couch cushions to construct a big foam rubber structure for you to climb on instead?"

And I would have said: "Darling, it seems you and I are struggling with a telephone conflict. We need to brainstorm some solutions for how we can both use the telephone in a fair and democratic manner."

And I wouldn't have ever tackled rock music lyrics. Back then, I was still young enough to realize that kids hear just the beat and not the words.

Only adults are under the impression that songs are *about* something. My mother went through a panicky phase during the 1960s, and started attending Rock Music Lyrics Meetings. She would come home insisting that "Light My Fire" was about sex and that a song called "Live for Today" would keep me from saving my babysitting money for college.

I couldn't imagine what she was going on about. All I had ever been able to hear in those songs was "Come on baby, light my fire" and "Tra la la la la la, live for today."

She forbade me to listen to such songs, just in case their offensive messages would take root in my delicate psyche and I would become a sociopath with no money for college. She also didn't hesitate to limit my telephone calls to five minutes each. And you can just imagine what it would have been like if I had wanted to stand on the table.

But there you have it: the basic difference between raising kids then and now. There weren't any Pocket Guides on Parenting until my mother was safely out of her how-to-be-a-perfect-mother years.

I just know she would never have understood my friend Steve, who in 1980 elevated Child Coaxing into an art form. He and his 2-year-old daughter, Tanya, were the supreme examples of how it could take 22 hours of sheer reason to get a kid into a coat, out the door of the day care center, and into the car.

The other day-care parents would stand around in awe, watching as Steve coaxed and reasoned and cajoled, without so much as mussing a hair on his mustache or bringing a bead of sweat to his brow.

He had a way of saying, "Now, Tanya, you and I both know what our goals here are. . . . " that would give goose bumps to his audience. Sometimes we would break into a round of applause.

But those days of wimpish parenting are gone.

Now that I've broken the barrier and said these three wrong things and no one died from it, I might even try out my mother's old favorite: "Keep up your crying, child, and I'll give you something to cry about!"

I don't know what it means, but then again, I never was very good at lyrics.

My True Calling

Lunch in New York

When you're a free-lance writer, you have two main jobs: making sure that no dust ever settles between the keys of your computer, and making sure that the doorknobs of your office are immaculately clean. But every now and then, an editor calls you up and wants to get together with you. In person.

The editor will say in a breezy tone of voice: "Why don't you come into the city on Thursday, and we'll have lunch?"

This sounds lovely. It *is* lovely. But usually it means that you are going to have to change out of your Lucky Writing Bathrobe, let the dust fall on your keyboard for a day, and actually go to New York. If like me, you have lived with children for too long, you will realize in New York that you don't understand what anything on the restaurant menu means.

And then, in addition to ordering mystery food (things with names like *gravlax en croute a l'orange*) and smiling a lot at your editor, you will be expected to make sense when you talk.

This is tough if you spend most of your time with kids. As my friend Sue, a writer who has gone through many lunches with editors, tells me: The two most important things are *not* to cut up the editor's food for her, and make sure you have something to talk about besides Barney. Many editors don't admire Barney as much as you do.

Lovely though the whole idea is, I have to say that the first time I got invited to the city for lunch with an editor was the most nerve-wracking day of my life. For one thing, I had a six-week-old baby, which means that I was in that rather delicate condition of bursting into tears whenever life seemed the slightest bit sad, which was most of the time. McDonald's commercials, for instance, made me wild with grief—especially the one where the little boy is separated from his dog all day long, but then after school they share a hamburger. This one still gets to me.

Also I was breast-feeding on a schedule of 30 minutes of nursing every 40 minutes, 24 hours a day. I knew, without even asking, that it wouldn't do to go into a New York restaurant with a person stuck to me—so I said yes, I would come, and then I hung up the phone and burst into tears.

There was plainly only one solution, and that was having my husband come with me. I would nurse the baby on the train, and then, while I dashed in and had lunch with the editor, my husband would walk the streets of New York, wearing the baby on his chest, tucked into the Snugli.

"I'm sure she'll just go back to thinking she's a fetus again and sleep the whole time," I told him.

Well, of course she didn't nurse for one second on the train. She slept the whole time—and by the time we got into New York, I was late for my lunch and had to run.

"Good luck!" he called to me, but I knew he'd be the one needing it.

The editor turned out to be a very classy, talkative New York-type, who loved telling funny stories and seemed to have nothing else to do for the rest of the afternoon but tell me all her stories and listen to all of mine.

We walked to a Japanese restaurant near the magazine's offices. On the way there, I thought I caught a glimpse of my husband in the crowd.

We ordered sushi, and talked as though we'd known each other all our lives. I was lying about how rosy life was with a new baby when suddenly, through the window, I saw my husband shuffling past, just as the editor asked, "And where is the baby today?"

I couldn't tell her. For one thing, I got so hysterical at the sight of my husband that I gulped down a whole wad of green horseradish and spent the next few minutes with my eyes and nose rubberbanding in and out of my face.

And since I didn't tell her then, of course, I couldn't *ever* tell her, especially not during the other three times he happened to pass by the window. Each time he looked more harried and desperate than before. In my over-heated, horseradish-inflamed brain, I wouldn't have been surprised if he'd stopped and pressed his face against the restaurant window, screaming my name.

Finally, hours later, she and I talked about story ideas, and she gave me some assignments. When we walked outside, she said, "We'll have to do this more often. It's so great that you have reliable child care and can come into the city so easily."

I said goodbye quickly.

I had to. My husband, with the baby shrieking in the Snugli, was heading our way.

Home Office

Everywhere you look these days, some magazine or other is recommending that you stop going to work and turn your home into an office.

"Work at home!" they say. "Get a fax machine and a modem, and you'll never have to see your co-workers again!"

Believe me, this is not a good idea.

I think everyone *really* knows, deep down, that a home can't be an office. Home is the place where, if you feel like cleaning a bathtub, there's one that probably could use it.

And, trust me, when you work at home, you'll come to think of an unclean bathtub as the only thing standing between you and Total Productivity.

No one knows for sure why this is, but there you will be, tapping your pencil on your desk and saying to yourself, "I just can't accomplish *anything* with that bathtub in the shape it's in!"

So you will get up out of your desk chair, arm yourself with rags and cleanser, and scrub at the tub as if mankind's very survival depended on the outcome. But, believe me, there is always one maddening little place that really needs something more: some cleaning product so expensive that you don't already have it in the house.

So you must go to the store to buy it. You must. Mankind's survival and all that. Then you stop off and get lunch someplace (after all, you have to support the local economy), and while you're there, you remember you have nothing for dinner, so you go to the grocery store to buy a chicken. Two hours later, you find yourself just completing the week's shopping.

You make it back just in time to bask in seven minutes of Quality Productive Time.

Just do yourself a favor: on the way back to your desk, don't allow your gaze to fall on any doorknobs.

There is hardly a doorknob in North America that couldn't be improved by four or five hours spent polishing it, and who knows when mankind's survival will depend on shiny doorknobs?

I work at home for three days. And no, thank you, my bathtub is not clean, and neither are my doorknobs. I would have had to improve some to get to those items. Instead, as often as not, I find myself trying to work with all three of my children surrounding me.

These days, the oldest kid, age 18, has somehow already finished his school year and is merely biding his time waiting for his Real Life to start when he goes away to college in the fall. While he waits, he is baby-sitting in the morning for the 5-year-old and her friend, who are in afternoon kindergarten.

Technically speaking, the 5-year old does, in fact, leave the house each day, but she's just in half-day kindergarten, which, it turns out, is equal to about 13 minutes. The rest of her day is simply a process of misplacing and then refinding her shoes, school papers, and backpack—and, of course, tending to her main occupation, which is pointing out situations in life which are Not Fair.

The middle child, who's in ninth grade, has mono and spends her days drifting from one chair to another, except when she's sleeping.

After giving a cursory swipe to the bathtub and—well, OK so I dusted off the doorknob, but only the one nearest the computer—I give the children the slip and settle down to work.

Naturally, I first have to straighten up the desk, make sure all the pens are pointing in the same direction, and gaze for a moment out the window to watch the dogwood blossoms drift to the ground. (Anyone will tell you that when you work at home, Appreciating Nature is very important.)

It's just when I'm in the middle of a major telephone call actually having to do with work that my door bursts open and I am asked by my 5-year-old to judge which piece of cheese is larger than the other.

She would love to tell me a whole tragic story, which apparently involves someone trying to foist on her an inferior-sized bit of cheese compared to the one her friend was given. But I give her my fiercest look. I am, after all, working.

But then, *while I am talking on the phone*, I get the calipers out, measure the cheeses, and point to the bigger piece.

That's what the magazines don't tell you. You *can* work at home, but only if you don't mind a dirty tub *and* you keep a pair of calipers nearby.

Career Day

There's nothing that should strike more fear in the heart of the American worker than Career Day at an elementary school.

This is when you go tell a bunch of 9-year-olds how great your job is. By the time you leave, you're wishing you'd just stayed drunk in college, the way your roommate did.

I've seen this happen time and time again. Reasonably well-adjusted people go waltzing into a classroom, brimming with enthusiasm for their chosen professions, and, after a few brief questions, come to see that their lives are worthless shams, suitable only for the scrap heap.

I once saw a fireman practically on his knees pleading with children to believe him that fighting fires was the most exciting and important job on the planet—but it was no use; he admitted he hadn't ever saved a whole skyscraper, like in the movies.

So I'm sure you can imagine how little respect a newspaper reporter gets.

I always go marching into the classroom, heavily armed with anecdotes about the incredible things I've gotten to write about over the years—like the eggplant that was a dead ringer for Richard Nixon, for instance—and year after year, the first question they have for me is always the same.

"Have you met Michael Jackson?"

What *is* it with Michael Jackson that children think that, as a reporter, I should be in contact with him? Is it just that he's the most famous person anyone can think of—or is it that his legal problems have become so monumental that all reporters everywhere should be expected to have covered them?

I don't know, but this question always gets me uneasy. Faces fall when I have to admit that no, I have never met Mr. Jackson. That's when I know that the Nixon eggplant is not going to get the respect it deserves.

So then I launch into my very hilarious and fascinating story of the deer that once leapt into someone's living room window while the homeowner was making coffee. The guy turned around, you see, and there was a huge *deer* standing in his kitchen, with antlers as big as the dining room table—

A hand goes up in the back. "Do you get to see movies like 'Batman' before other people see them?"

"Um, no," I say. Before I can launch into my next story—a harrowing tale about a hen that laid a gigantic egg—someone else wants to know if I get to hang out much at the White House, and do I think it's possible for Chelsea Clinton to get a boyfriend with all those Secret Service men around?

By now, something in my eyes must be telegraphing: *Help!* Because usually this is the point where the teacher steps in and explains that I'm a reporter covering a local beat, and that my job is basically—here she looks at me questioningly, as if this might be a blank I would care to fill in.

It's at moments like this that you are shocked into a wretched understanding of what your life really amounts to. Clearly, it seems to these kids that my basic professional purpose is to inform the public about unusual-shaped vegetables and insane animals in their area. I glance desperately at the firefighter. He shrugs helplessly.

So I lamely try to tell them about my Most Exciting Investigation Ever, when I got a secret tip that a school board member had called his mother in Florida from the school board's phones, which led to an award-winning five-part series on corruption. Or the story I once did about the Sewer Commission's distress over some rock formations.

By now, some kids are looking like they've gone under anesthesia. Wildly, I search for something I've covered that a kid could respect.

"Wait, I did meet somebody famous once!" I say. "Luis from 'Sesame Street.'" Then I actually have to say, "You know, one of the *human* characters—brown hair, sings songs?" Someone laughs.

"So why *did* you go into journalism anyway?" a girl wants to know.

It would be ridiculous then to explain about Woodward and Bernstein and how a bunch of us were going to end corruption and cure politics and keep the public informed.

So I give my second-best reason: "You get to sleep late most days."

It's then that the firefighter stirs from his humiliated stupor and claims that was *his* reason too. Then we crawl back to work to hand in our resignations.

Computer Terminals

Say what you will about the state of American journalism today, but things are not going to get any better until word processors stop being hostile.

I myself have had a lifetime of being despised by machines, and am used to the way, say, a blender can casually toss squished-up carrots and tomatoes all over a kitchen with impunity. I also own a sewing machine that *insists* on being called every four-letter word you know before it will even consider sewing a seam. And for years I had to wear a raincoat while I drove, because my Plymouth Duster persisted in tossing mysterious fluids at me while we went down the road.

But even I, who was well aware of how insidious was the ground war between humans and machines, was unprepared for what awaited me in the newsroom.

The way it's supposed to work is this: reporters have at their desks their own computer terminals, as well as private electronic queues, where they keep the stories they're working on. When, against all odds, a story gets finished, the reporter pushes a button and sends it to one of the editing queues, where copy editors await it. These are people who were hired because of their ability to string together long lines of words that have no discernible meaning whatsoever, strings of words that they like to call "headlines." (My personal all-time favorite is: "Top Fizz Probe Cap Eyed.")

While reporters are going for coffee with their newsroom

friends, editors spend their days aimlessly patrolling these editing queues, looking up periodically to bark something like, "*Shelton!* Deadline is in six hours! Why don't I already have that story?"

Despite what you might think, the system works beautifully—or would, if technology didn't rear its ugly head.

But perhaps I am prejudiced. Before I started working at Big City Newspapers, I was the editor of a weekly paper, the kind with manual typewriters and old men in green visors in the back room with the hot type. There, when you finished a story, by golly, you had something you could hold in your hand. A piece of paper to call your own!

Not any more. These days, when the story gets finished, you type in which queue you want it to go to, press the SEND button, the screen goes blank, and you get ready to go home.

Except, if you're me, the editor says, "*Shelton!* Deadline came and went! Where is that story?"

Me: "I sent it!"

Editor: "Well, I didn't get it!"

Me: "Maybe it's stuck in the wires that run under the carpet."

That is clearly the only possible explanation. But because the newsroom higher-ups are unwilling to shred the carpeting in search of lost stories, I have spent too many nights rewriting them, and sometimes rewriting them again. I was once enthusiastically writing a travel guide to Cape Cod—screen after screen about all the wonderful things a person could do there; and when the computer swallowed this story for the *second* time, my third version read in its entirety: "Go to Cape Cod if you want to. It can be pretty nice sometimes."

But even that incident, bad as it was, isn't the worst of the wickedness that newsroom computers have perpetrated. They do their very worst in the realm of electronic mail. In fact, I think Congress really should require personnel managers to inform new employees that e-mail systems are to be used only if you want the entire world to know something.

Case in point: At one newspaper, a friend of mine, angry at a copy editor, once dashed off an e-mail note to another reporter, pointing out that the copy editor not only was a moron, but had piano legs, dragon breath, and hair that resembled a rodent on her head—and then pressed the wrong button and sent it flashing on everyone's screen across the newsroom.

A *very* bad technology day.

Then there was the copy editor who apparently grew so bored waiting for stories to come into his queue that he took up writing a racy novel in his spare time.

All the reporters enjoyed it immensely the day it mysteriously landed on their screens—especially the parts about people in the newsroom, thinly disguised, of course. Unfortunately, the city editor didn't have a good sense of humor—or maybe he didn't like the idea of himself in a tutu—so the copy editor/novelist got fired.

They don't call them "terminals" for nothing, you know.

Queen of the PTA

In one short year of working at home, I've learned a lot about life.

The main thing I've learned is that anytime you're at home, the PTA doesn't see why you can't be baking them some cupcakes.

After all, it wouldn't *kill* you to have the oven on while you're typing, would it? And how long does it take to break a few eggs into a bowl? You could do it on your next trip to the mirror, the very next time you need to make sure your teeth stayed straight all these years after orthodontia.

Making sure of your teeth's straightness is extremely important, and people who work in offices aren't able to devote the time to it that it requires. It's a little-known fact that even 30 years after being straightened, teeth still remember the good old days when they got to lodge every which-way in your gums, and slowly—very slowly—they're creeping back to that point.

Possibly you're thinking you can keep track of your dental movements, get your work done, *and* bake cupcakes, all in a single day, but I'm sorry, this is not possible in one lifetime. The truth is that baking *any* kind of cupcake for *anyone* is so much more gratifying than writing on any given day that pretty soon you'll be happily running a cupcake factory, and soon your paychecks will stop and your children won't have clothes to wear to school, and what's worse, you won't be able to buy any more cupcake ingredients.

No, no. There's no future in cupcakes. Not for *you*.

But while we're on the subject of the PTA's cupcakes, you might as well know that that first cupcake request is really just a big test, to see if you're the kind of person they can then get to *run* the whole bake sale. Say yes, and in no time you will be running their spring fair, organizing rallies, putting on rummage sales and talent shows—and then they'll give you some great title like Chief Executive Manager/Queen of the PTA World, and you'll end up having to go to all their meetings and be in charge of guilt-tripping everyone else into baking cupcakes—and your friends will try to hide from you when they see you coming.

Noooo thank you. My teeth are starting to slide back at an alarming rate, and besides that, I'm on permanent deadline at the newspaper. Incredible as it may seem, something is due every half-hour for the next 20 or 30 years.

This brings me to the second thing I've learned from working at home: you will have to cultivate a specialized phone voice for talking to people who call you up and want you to do things, especially your editor, who will call you more times each day than you can believe.

Trust me: It does not behoove you to pick up the phone and sing out, "Helloooo" in your usual, chatty, enthusiastic way, even if you are out of your mind with gratitude that the phone has just rung and you can talk to another human being and finally stop trying to figure out why you really *didn't* make a career choice that involved baking cupcakes, and whether it's not too late to switch, and if your new career would pay for new braces for your teeth, should it come to this.

But it's *not* another human being. It's your editor, and he wants to know many things: when is that story going to be ready, why didn't you already send in the photo assignment, what will you be working on for next week, why did you spell that woman's name such a weird way in the story, and on and on.

The voice you want to strive for here communicates many things.

It says: "No, I have *not* been making cupcakes or checking my teeth. I've been right here working hard all morning."

It says: "I'm a highly organized, competent worker who is *swamped* with interviews and really too busy right now to talk to you, and of course I can spell names correctly!"

Mostly it says: "How do you expect me to get any real work done if you're always talking to me on the phone?!"

Soon, if you are lucky and have mastered the proper voice intonations, your editor will stop bugging you, the PTA will go off and forget about the cupcakes you could have made, and you can have some peace and quiet in front of the computer screen. You know, get a little work done.

But don't worry. The school bus will be along to save you any minute now.

Much More Than
I'll Ever Know

Halloween

By the time you read this, I expect I will have gone over the edge into complete insanity, another victim of the Halloween Candy Syndrome.

It seemed like such a good idea at the time: allowing the children to dress up in funny costumes and go door to door, saying "Trick or Treat" and collecting bags full of candy.

I completely forgot about the part where the candy stays on for days and days, and becomes the sole subject of conversation in the house.

We don't say "Good morning" to each other in our house anymore. The first conversation of the day instead goes like this:

Kid: "Can I have a piece of candy?"
Parent: "No. You haven't had breakfast."
Kid: "Can I have *three* pieces of candy?"
Parent: "No. You haven't had breakfast."
Kid: "What about *five* pieces of candy?"
Parent: "OK. One piece of candy."
Kid: "No. Six."

What I want to know is this: where do these kids learn their negotiation skills anyway? And would it help or hurt our cause if we deployed some 3-year-olds to the Mideast to handle the peace talks?

I should have known it was going to be a nightmare of a Halloween from the moment we set out trick-or-treating with

Stephanie, our 3-year-old fairy princess. First of all, none of our other children would be seen with us.

The 15-year-old said he was too old for Candy Acquisition and would instead dress as a Mafia boss and give out lollipops at our house. He had some scheme for extorting candy from young kids who came to the door, but we discouraged this.

The 12-year-old, dressed in a poodle skirt and cashmere sweater, disappeared with her friends, talking about James Dean and Chubby Checker. She was headed to a party that promised to provide tons of candy to her cause.

I figured we'd be done in five or six minutes.

"I think Stephanie will be too scared to go to very many houses," I whispered to my husband. This, after all, is a kid who has been known to claim that a room lit by a mere 60-watt bulb is too dark for an unescorted child to enter. Monsters, you know, can thrive in any room with wattage less than 100.

I had her pegged all wrong.

She brazenly charged up to porches where there were actual Card-Carrying Witches cackling and threatening children with bodily harm if they came one step farther.

"I think there's really special candy once you get past the witch," she told us.

It was this kind of at-any-cost attitude that landed us home one hour later with a haul that guaranteed a lifetime of hyperactivity and dextrose overload.

I quickly slipped into my Mom-of-the-'90s Mode, separating the loot into the standard five piles: the Possibly Poisoned Candies, recognizable by their torn wrappers; the Possibly Razor-Blade Laden Fruits; the Chokables, like peanuts and gumdrops; the Wonderfully Scrumptious Chocolates Meant for the Parents; and the Kid Pile, composed almost entirely of Raisinets (a health food, by Halloween standards).

The kid was outraged.

She immediately started negotiating for as many pieces as she could possibly consume before bedtime. We settled on three.

Her first choice was a pack of Necco wafers containing 35 candies. Then a bag of chocolate candies with M's on them.

Then a bag of candy corn. In all, hundreds of pieces of candy were disappearing into her mouth. But was she satisfied with this coup she had pulled off?

No. We started right in on the philosophical question that has perplexed thinkers for centuries: Is Gum Candy?

Since then, our time has been taken up with even weightier questions, like: Is a Peanut Butter Candy More Nutritionally Valuable than a Lollipop? What Is Candy Corn Made Of, and Why Does the Company Bother? And of course, the main one: How Much Candy Is Owed to the Person Who Stayed Home Handing Out Candy and Is Now Sorry?

But my personal favorite remains: Why Didn't We Just Throw All the Candy Away?

Pogs

To those of you who have been concerned about us, let me assure you: our family now has acquired some pogs.

We have finally stepped into the 1990s.

My 6-year-old daughter, Stephanie, couldn't be more relieved. She came home from school the other day and reported that we were the objects of pity among her friends.

"Everyone in school has had pogs for weeks and weeks," she said. "They ask me, 'Where are your pogs?' and I don't know how to tell them that I don't have even one pog."

"Wait a minute," I said. "Back up! What exactly is a pog, anyway?"

She got a vague, faraway look on her face. "It's a round thing," she said.

This was a lot of help.

I called up my friend Lynne, whose daughter is on the cutting edge of fashion.

"Do you have a pog?" I asked her.

"Of course!" she said. "We have many pogs."

"Well, then, would you tell me what they are?"

After she stopped laughing at me, she started trying to get me to believe that pogs are little cardboard disks that have pictures on them and that, once upon a time, were probably cousins to caps that went to milk bottles, back when milk came in bottles.

"Why does my child want these?" I asked.

"Why does *anyone's* child want these?" she asked. "No one knows for sure."

Then I understood. This was the Latest Rage. It was like hoola hoops and pet rocks.

The next day, Stephanie and I happened to be in the car, and suddenly she let out a shriek that made my blood run immediately down into my toes and stay there. We had just passed a store, she said, that had a huge fluorescent sign in the window saying: "We Have Pogs."

"It's the We Have Pogs store!" she shouted. "All the kids have told me about this store! This is where pogs come from!"

You might as well know this about me right now: I have very little character and heaps of curiosity, so I pulled into the We Have Pogs parking lot, and she and I ran into the store, just in case the pog craze would end before we made our purchases.

We were lucky. The saleswoman there said the pog craze was as strong as ever and would certainly be extended at least until the end of the week, as far as anyone could tell.

So then we relaxed and started examining bags and bags of pogs.

If you are thinking of joining the pog craze, be prepared to do some deep thinking about your life first. It would help, in fact, if you had a psychoanalyst along to explain certain of your personality traits. You won't believe the number of decisions you have to make before you can buy even one pog.

For instance, are you the glitzy sort? If so, then you want the more expensive holographic pogs. Or perhaps you go in for heavy metal music, in which case you might need the pogs decorated with skulls that have snakes crawling out of the eyeball sockets. Or maybe you're the Barney type.

The saleswoman said, "I'll leave you two alone. I don't bother pog shoppers."

We sifted through bag after bag. We knew we weren't glitzy, and we knew we weren't heavy metal exactly—and God forbid we should regress back to our Barney phase.

"None of these are just right," said Stephanie finally. "I don't know *who* I am."

I knew just how she felt. I have often been faced with this type of realization—but usually it is when I'm trying on bathing suits.

In the end, we went for some cartoonish sort of pogs—light hearted, with a dash of *je ne sais quios.*

She explained that we'd then be needing a "slammer," which is apparently what you're supposed to hit the pogs with. It's not a game if you don't hit the pogs, she told me.

After another eternity of soul-searching, we settled on a yin-yang design of slammer, a metal one with sparkles.

I sighed with relief when we could finally leave. I felt we knew ourselves much better than when we came in.

I have to admit that we're still not sure what you actually *do* with pogs once you've selected them.

Only the puppy has a clear idea of what they're good for. He says they're delicious as an appetizer.

Happy Campers

Something funny happens to kids in the summer. If they're not drooping over the furniture moaning about how there's nothing to do, it's probably because some institution has transformed them into Campers.

And Campers, as parents soon realize, are a different breed of person from the usual kid they have knocking around the house all year.

They are important. They are organized. And they know how to make lanyards.

Never mind that no people in their right minds will wear lanyards. Campers produce them by the dozens. At a really good camp, they can make as many as 10 lanyards *each day*, in practically any color you can imagine.

In fact, the biggest decision a camper has to make each day is whether Aunt Elizabeth would like her latest lanyard to be raspberry pink with olive green or something more hip, like passionate purple with fluorescent orange. And at every camp, there are some forward-thinking campers who realize that by December, their friends and families will be clamoring for red and green Christmas lanyards, so they make up a few dozen in that color combination before summer is out.

There is hardly a camper alive who doesn't immediately realize that this lanyard-making skill is going to solve a lot of gift-giving problems in the future. So what that it's another year until Father's Day pops up again—Dad will need a couple of business-suit-type lanyards (navy blue and maroon are popular) for when he has meetings to go to.

But making lanyards is just *one* of the many skills children acquire when they join the world of Campers. They also learn Facts of Nature.

These facts are very important for children to know, and they are happy to pass them on to you every time you are near anything even resembling nature, for the next 30 years.

"I'll bet you didn't know that's nature's toothbrush," they will tell you every single time there is a birch tree anywhere about. "If you're lost in the woods, you can use a twig of that tree to freshen your breath."

At camp, you learn that fresh breath is important to people wandering, lost, in the woods. But wait, there is more.

"Did you know that dandelions are edible?"

"Did you know that if you pour water on the leaves of a certain plant, it looks like silver money?"

"Did you know that if 50 people all clap their hands very softly, it sounds like rain?"

These are not the kind of facts you can learn in just any schoolroom. It takes a camp counselor to impart such wisdom.

And there's another thing that only camp counselors can accomplish: They achieve perfect discipline and cooperation through a system of bead-giving. It's just too bad our penal system doesn't know about it.

This is how it works: Each day you show up at camp, you get a bead. You do something really great, like drink your Hi-C without spilling it—you get another bead. Shoot the arrow toward the target instead of at your friend Larry—you guessed it, another bead.

If you're a medium-terrific kid who has minimal motor control skills and isn't a sociopath, there is no end to the number of beads you can own by the end of a two-week stint at camp. And everyone wears them around their necks, proudly. You are in fine company at camp when you sport some lanyards and bead necklaces.

At camp, also, it seems they really understand your true

identity. They put you in a group of other like-minded fun-seekers and call the whole lot of you "otters" or "turtles" or some such thing. It fits. It works. You like it.

But just as you're really getting into the idea of being one of nature's turtles, it ends. That's it. Camp's over.

The magic wears off slowly. It dawns on you quite gradually that no one around the house remembers that you earned 37 beads for being wonderful, and that Aunt Elizabeth hasn't been wearing her lanyard lately.

Luckily you can still go to the park and gather some of nature's toothbrushes. They can't take that away from you.

Parents' Night

It's Parents' Night at day camp, and my 7-year-old daughter, Stephanie, has given me careful instructions on what to wear and how to behave.

Believe me, I am as shocked as you are that these instructions are deemed necessary. But apparently in the past I have misbehaved at public functions and, from now on, I will have to be informed of the Rules of Deportment before I can go anywhere.

"I hate to hurt your feelings," she says to me, "but when you come to the camp, could you please make sure about a few things?"

"Sure," I say. I am thinking she maybe would like me to bring her sweatshirt in case it has turned cold.

You would probably think a woman with three children would know by now that there has never been a child in the whole world who anticipates getting cold later and hopes to have a sweatshirt brought along. *That* is how little I have learned in the past 19 years.

And no, this is not what she wants this time either. Instead, I am given a recounting of The Official Rules of Parents' Night:

1. I am *not* to cheer or call out, "The Leaping Leopards are the best tribe in this whole camp!"

(This is because I am suspected of being the person at Stephanie's dance recital last spring who shouted, "An encore from the Water Creatures!" while the dancers were bowing.)

(Of *course* that wasn't me.)

2. Also: I am to wear the blue and yellow lanyard necklace that she made for me at camp, but I am *not* to show off or brag to the other mothers about it.

3. If people specifically request more information about this lanyard, I may modestly admit that yes, Stephanie selected the colors.

4. And that I have a key chain just like it.

5. Also with colors selected by Stephanie.

6. As for my wearing apparel besides the lanyard necklace, I should wear jeans because I will probably have to sit on the ground. Under no circumstances am I to wear a skirt or a dress. This is camp, she tells me, not a *party*.

7. Would it be too much to ask that I wear my hair down and not pinned back in a barrette, as I've been doing these past few hot days?

8. And if I *must* wear a barrette, would I please *not* wear that silly-looking barrette with the colored beads on it, but could I wear the more dignified tortoise-shell colored one instead?

9. I am absolutely *not* to wear a hat—especially the dorky white floppy one with the pink silk flowers on the side.

10. If I see a snake at camp, I am to ignore it and not scream or jump around and make a spectacle of myself.

11. If I see a spider, however, I should surreptitiously kill it without any camp personnel seeing me because at camp they actually think spiders are good

and refuse to do away with them, even if they are currently threatening to crawl on Stephanie.

12. Last, I shouldn't sing louder than the other parents during the sing-along around the campfire.

Well, I don't mind telling you I was stunned. Stunned!

All this from the person who, as we passed the sausages in the Stop & Shop meat department, once screamed out: "Why do they sell CAT POOP in this store?"

And it's from the same person who once threw up all over me just as the airplane was taking off, jam-packed, and although we had a change of clothes for *her* in the diaper bag, we didn't have a change of clothes for *me* and so I had to smell like sour milk for four hours, and everyone moved to other parts of the plane to get away from us.

And the same person who came flouncing out of a public rest room and announced to a crowded restaurant, at the top of her lungs: "I wouldn't even sit on that potty, it was so *dirty* and *misgusting*!"

That person?

The same one who stood up in her stroller one day at the bank and said, "Dame it! I hate waiting in line!"

I have to tell you I'm tempted to put on a skirt, the beaded barrette, my flowered hat, and join in, full-blast, during the sing-along. And afterward I'll say, "BY GOSH, THOSE LEAPING LEOPARDS ARE THE MOST INCREDIBLE TRIBE EVER, RIGHT FOLKS?"

I would, but I've still got the teen years to get through.

Family Member Scores Goal

I don't want to get any sports talent scouts too excited or anything, but a member of our family has scored a goal in soccer.

Yes, it's true. Stephanie, who is seven, has ended what may be a five-generation slump in Sports Scoring.

Before this, the closest we'd come to having anyone score a point in an athletic contest was 12 years ago when, during an otherwise listless Little League game, my son got a walk. His teammates and their parents were so amazed by his refusal to swing the bat that they gave him a standing ovation. Naturally, he grinned and tipped his hat to the crowd while he sauntered down the base line to first.

I thought I knew the limit of parental athletic pride *then*, but let me tell you: that was nothing compared to *now*. Now our family has an actual *point* to its credit. We have made a numerical contribution to a real *game*.

So now, as I see it, the all-time score is: Our Family: 1. All The Other Scorers We've Played Against In The Last Five Generations: 2,687.

But it's a start.

I just wish Mrs. Wentz, my seventh grade physical education teacher, could have been there. Not that she knew from soccer, of course. This was the '60s, when the highest aspirations of P.E. teachers mostly had to do with Jumping Jacks.

Day after day, she had us outside, standing in military-straight lines, jumping our jacks while we counted out loud. I didn't mind. I would stand out there by the hour, if necessary, mindlessly jumping up and down, flapping my arms, just pleased that nobody was keeping score.

But then, sometime during the semester, it would occur to Mrs. Wentz that you can't have a year in which nobody gets to make any points—and then we would have to have a Game.

Back in seventh grade, getting ready for a game meant learning pages of rules. And then, after we'd been properly tested and grilled on the rules, Mrs. Wentz, by some mysterious process, would choose team captains—and then, by an even *more* mysterious process, those captains would select teammates.

This, you might as well know right now, is when I developed my very first neurosis.

Even today, I don't quite know how I was immediately identified as Someone Who Would Sink the Team's Chances, but I was. It's true that I was already predestined to close my eyes when I was at bat and to forget to dribble the basketball while I ran with it—but that's not the point. The point is: how did *they* know?

Nobody ever wanted to pick me for her team, and finally Mrs. Wentz would have to step in and *make* someone take me, usually, I think, in exchange for extra points—but at least once I think it might have involved a cash reward.

Then the captain would place me way out in the outfield, so far away that it was possible to forget there was even a game going on somewhere in the same zip code. Certainly the *ball* never came that far.

Once I remember realizing the school buses had come and taken everybody home, and I was still in the outfield, wearing my gym suit, waiting for some action to come my way. Okay, so I had sat down and looked for four-leaf clovers for a while—so what? If my team had needed me, I could have been ready.

That day Mrs. Wentz had a little talk with me about my attitude and suggested that maybe the next year I'd be more suited for a class like Modern Dance. She said all a person would have to do was be willing to flit around in the gymnasium while soft music played.

I said, "Do they keep score in modern dance? Is it something you can *lose* at?"

Mrs. Wentz looked at me for a long time, and then said it was exactly that kind of attitude that could hold me back in life. I wanted to tell her then about the four scoreless generations before me, and how *nobody*—nobody—in my family had ever so much as caught a ball tossed their way.

I didn't think she'd get it.

But now we have a scorer in the family. Somebody has actually made a ball go where it was supposed to, and turned and flashed a dazzling smile.

Well, it made me wish that just once I could have come in closer from the outfield.

The Sphinx

If anyone had asked me, this was *not* the time I would have chosen to make a model of the Sphinx.

I was already fully booked up by the washing machine, which had decided it would be fun to drain water on the basement floor. And the oil burner, not to be outdone, had figured out how to spurt water out of all its valves at one time.

I'm sorry, but when you have *two* lakes competing daily in the basement, you do not ask yourself if it's time you buckled down and got to work on your own personal model of the Sphinx.

But the New Haven public school system felt it was time I put down those buckets and mops and got down to the real business of living. Enough of our Sphinxless existence.

They sent word home with my 12-year-old daughter, Allie, that a model of the Sphinx would be required practically immediately.

No more procrastination. No more would I have to be embarrassed at cocktail parties when people inquired where my Sphinx was. I was going to get one pretty fast.

This, after all, is one of the main purposes of the school system—to think up School Projects That The Whole Family Can Become Involved In.

Teachers deny this, of course. They will say they intended only for the child to be employed in the project. "You can just keep living your life, mopping up your basement," they will tell you. "Your kid is perfectly capable of making a Sphinx all alone."

I don't know what children they could possibly be referring to. *My* children, when it is School Project Time, go into thick, dark depressions. They mope around the house. They drape themselves across the furniture. They develop Symptoms.

"I have to make a model," they say piteously, "and I don't know what to make it out of."

I always start out the same doggedly optimistic way, year after year. "Draw a picture," I say. You'd think I'd know that this suggestion will never be accepted.

There's something about the still-developing, immature mind of a child that causes it to gravitate only toward the elaborate—some would say impossible—genre of School Project. They need materials that can only be gleaned from the farthest reaches of the solar system, or the top-secret laboratories of NASA.

As a veteran of many years of School Projects, I can't tell you how many times I have actually stood in hardware stores and argued with clerks that there *must* be materials in the world that can create a miniature, working hovercraft that operates on lasers.

"Sell me some laser beams!" I shouted to one particularly obstinate clerk. "I know you have them!"

Once, my son was given the assignment to create a working robot, using a coil of copper wire, a phonograph record, and a piece of wood.

And then there was the year we toiled, night after night, to create an authentic cathedral in a shoe box. After that, I was tempted to include on my resume that I once outfitted an entire package of wooden clothespins in authentic medieval costumes.

Over the years, there have been requests for endless dioramas with genuine exploding volcanoes, and relief maps that required all the cornstarch we could find in three towns. The worst time was when my son wanted to motorize some raisins, so they would accurately represent newborn puppies.

Compared with all this, I suppose a model of a Sphinx should seem easy.

"Maybe I could make it out of Ivory soap," says Allie. "Oh, but how could I make it tall enough?"

My friend Edith, unfailingly sympathetic now that she's got her kids tucked away in diorama-free universities, suggests we glue two bars of soap together.

I thank her profusely, but I am glaring the whole time.

Later in the week I run into Allie's teacher. Jokingly I say, "You've ruined my life with this model of the Sphinx business, you know."

Her eyes widen. "Oh, she doesn't have to make a model," she says. "She actually picked that. There were other options."

Whoa. Could there be hope here?

"She could have made a slide show of the Sphinx," says the teacher.

Damn, I'll bet the flights to Egypt are already booked this week.

Marching Into Tomorrow

I cry at graduations.

I don't know what it is about the sight of people wearing little mortarboards with tassels, but I've been known to burst into tears at the sight of total strangers heading across the street to their graduation ceremonies.

And once the music starts playing, and people get up and make speeches about Marching On Into Tomorrow—well, trust me, I'm the one on the floor, wailing and pounding her fists.

So I expected to do it all again when my son Ben graduated from high school.

I sat in a metal folding chair in the sun, a wad of Kleenex in both hands.

My mother-and father-in-law and husband were on one side of me, and my two daughters, my sister, and ex-husband were on the other side. It was a hot day, and I had spent it racing around buying film and doing laundry, cleaning the house for company, and cooking. I had been grouchy.

Later, I saw that by being grouchy, I was trying to steel myself against falling apart at graduation. I didn't want to cry in front of all those people. I wanted to be one of those moms who smile and say, "Wow! I didn't think this day would ever come!"

They didn't play "Pomp and Circumstance." The graduates entered to "What a Wonderful World" sung by Louis Armstrong. When Ben passed by my row, Louis Armstrong was singing the part about, "I see babies cry, I watch them grow. They'll learn much more than I'll ever know."

My chin wobbled.

A teacher got up and made a short speech. He's an old friend of mine, one of the fathers from the cooperative day care we belonged to when our kids were little. Lately, I've run into him at the high school and we've talked, not only about old times, but about colleges and test scores.

He looked out at the crowd and told us our babies were ready to fly away. "And after you fly away," he said to the graduates, "I hope you'll also fly back sometimes and come see us again. We like to see how you've grown up."

I blew my nose.

Graduation from high school is just a moment in time, I told myself—just a snapshot in which we stop for a minute and notice that time has passed, that those who were little have grown up around us. It's a rite of passage in a culture that no longer has very many left.

The graduates—those who wanted to—took turns getting up at the microphone and saying goodbye. Some wept. One girl said she had been taking college courses all year and hadn't been around the high school much lately. "I went back there this week to say goodbye, and found out I couldn't," she said, her voice breaking. "So that's what I'm doing now."

The sun went down, a breeze fluttered, and the evening took on the warm, intimate feel of a party. One by one, graduates came to the microphone to speak about leaving high school. Some were funny and silly and made the audience laugh in appreciation. Others looked out over the heads of their parents and friends and plainly spoke of how difficult their teen years had been, and how the love from friends and teachers had sustained them.

One young woman was joined by her toddler daughter at the microphone, and together they smiled out at the crowd while we cheered the young mom for making it through school.

At the end of the ceremony, the class of '94 threw their caps in the air, in that moment that perhaps best symbolizes graduations everywhere: inner-city, rural, suburban, old-fashioned and right now.

I drifted back through the crowd.

There were all the people I knew best when I first moved to New Haven when Ben was a baby: friends that I used to see daily at day care but lately have only seen at school functions. Joanie had long ago helped me figure out how to get Ben to sleep through the night. Lynne and I had clung to each other on the first day of kindergarten, until the teacher had made us leave. Liddy had helped me through my divorce.

Ben was hugging his teachers and saying goodbye. He was smiling and saying he'd come back and visit.

But what I hadn't expected was that I was saying goodbye too, to people I know I won't run into anymore. We said we'll call each other, but I bet we won't. That era was ending for us right then.

We have to March On Into Tomorrow too.

An Astonishing and
Refreshing Decade

The Mailing List
for Crazy People

I haven't wanted to talk to anyone about this, but the fact is that I have somehow gotten myself on the Mailing List for Crazy People.

Day after day, I go out to my mailbox, and instead of the usual collection of household bills and letters from banks who want me to ruin my credit-rating by owning still *more* MasterCards, there are letters with bright red words splashed all across them, saying things like: "Lies! Lies! Lies! All seats on an airplane are not equally safe! And your insurance agent is not looking out for your best interests! Look inside for even more lies!"

Normally I am not a person who looks around for even more lies. It's just not one of my interests. So for a while, I was just throwing all this stuff in the garbage without even opening it.

This is where having children around the house can really come in handy.

There is not a kid in America who doesn't act as a powerful magnet for this kind of stuff, and sure enough, pretty soon all my junk mail was being magnetized right out of the garbage can and landing right back in my lap, brought there by an eager-faced kid.

I had no idea what I was missing.

But let me tell you: the quality of my junk mail has very suddenly taken a dramatic turn toward the lunatic fringe.

Somehow the word has gotten out that I am a major loser

in dire need of help of every description, and there is no scam outfit on the planet that isn't willing to get that help for me.

Even the World's Foremost Mentalist, "The Amazing" Kreskin, has taken the time to write to me—not once but twice—because he's so frantic about my personal situation.

He claims to *know* I can succeed in life, if I will just send him money for six of his secrets. He has even put himself on the line here and identified me as someone who has "special mental potential." He senses that I am one of the chosen ones on Earth who can get others to do what I want them to do.

Possibly he's not realizing that I am a person who cannot even get junk mail to stay in the garbage can.

Most of the folks writing me letters, though, are more concerned about my health than my powers of persuasion.

Not a day goes by that someone new doesn't write me about some new mysterious miracle food I should be eating *every day* if I'd like to restore my former eye color, cure any arthritis I might be having, and keep myself cancer-free for life. The secret seems to be a "shunned herb" from Europe that I can find out the name of if I will only send a lot of dollars.

I am all for this shunned herb making its way back into public favor, but my question is this: What are they talking about with this *former* eye color stuff?

What in the world happens to eye color?

So now I know what's going to happen: This will be some new thing to worry about during those times when I'm sitting at my word processor trying to process words that will not be produced.

Instead of jumping up and polishing the doorknobs, now I'll have to go check my eye color in the mirror to decide if it's the same eye color I had a few days ago, or if it's going. At night, I'll be asking my husband, "So, do you think my eyes are the same color as when you left this morning?"

But the worst of the junk mail came today—an impassioned letter from a psychic named Irene who has an alarming gut feeling that things just aren't right with me, that I have a serious personal problem that is *eating away at me*.

She's not sure exactly what it is; she would need $19.95 before she could think harder about it than she already is. But she hints that a Cadillac could be in my future if I get involved in her "destiny program."

And, she says, she has seen that there were actually a few times in my life when I came close to real happiness.

I'm surprised she knew about those times.

I remember them well. It was back when my junk mail was just boring letters from banks and life insurance companies that probably didn't have my best interests at heart.

Back before I knew about that poor little shunned herb, and that my eye color is going to fade.

I was so happy and innocent then.

Driving Injustices

I sat quietly in my car and watched the traffic light go through two cycles of red-green-yellow.

This was a very Zen thing for me to do, you understand.

But, truthfully, it wasn't my choice. The car in front of me was not going to move. The car's driver was conducting his romantic life with a front-seat passenger, and somehow the two of them had forgotten what you're supposed to do when the light turns green.

So I sat there and waited.

I practiced deep breathing. Then I *counted* my deep breaths. I read all the billboards and studied the local architecture. After a while, I revved the engine, hoping this would serve as a gentle reminder. Then, later, I tapped on the steering wheel in time to the four or five songs that played on the radio throughout this little Vacation from Driving.

When the light turned green for the *third* time, I leaned my head out of the window and resorted to pleading. "Won't you *please*, please, please go this time?"

This is what life is like when your car horn breaks.

It's amazing what that little "beep beep" does for you. It communicates worlds of meaning, everything from Won't-you-please-go-now-that-the-light-has-changed to Watch-it-you-big-lug-you're-getting-in-my-lane.

Without it, I've had to develop a whole new driving personality.

I've had to actually become *nice*.

This has not been easy for me.

Oh, I used to be a nice driver, back when I lived in California. There, by state statute, you can get a traffic ticket just for failing to be excruciatingly polite.

In fact—and this may come as something of a shock to the drivers in my town—in California they *don't allow cars to knock down the pedestrians*. And not just the pedestrians on the sidewalks either. Trust me on this one: if you are driving a car and people step off the curb and cross the street in front of you, you are *still* not allowed to hit them.

Another law they have is that you can't just change lanes whenever you feel like it. I know they can't enforce anything like that in Connecticut where I live, because the entire population would have to go to jail and the jails are already too full. But in California somehow they've convinced drivers that it's a good idea to turn on their turn signal and look in the rear view mirror before they hop over to somebody else's lane.

I know, I know. It's a radical state.

But I used to drive like that. When I lived in California, I would rather sit forever at a stop sign than take a chance of going when it wasn't my democratically agreed-upon turn. In fact, I've actually seen out-of-car conferences taking place at four-way stops while Californians tried to sort out their order of arrival.

Now that I'm in New Haven, I've changed, of course. These days I know I'm putting my fellow drivers' lives in jeopardy when I'm the first car to stop after the light turns red. This causes at least four cars to swerve around me as they try to pass.

And forget the ritual of deciding who goes first at a stop sign. The one who goes first is the one who runs it.

When I first moved here, a friend of mine explained Stop Sign Etiquette this way: If you ever want your turn, pretend you don't see any other cars, press on the gas and hope.

It's rude, she said, to depend on other drivers to take the extra step of waiting for you to go. Takes up their precious time.

Same for pedestrians. As my friend explained, it's best not to confuse them by letting them walk in front of your car while you wait at the corner: This only lulls them into a false sense of security, and then the driver behind you will be forced to go out of his way to teach them a lesson.

I miss my horn.

Sitting by quietly while Driving Injustices take place is really not my style.

Maybe, until I can get an appointment to get it fixed, I should invest in a bullhorn. I could lean out the window and yell: "You there! That light's been green for one whole second! Now get with it!"

Or maybe it's a good time to introduce the California Approach.

"How many of you think the red car was first, and how many think the green car was?"

The Most Fun Toy Contest

I have some bad news for the toy manufacturers of America: kids are not playing with your toys.

It's not that you don't come up with some cute ideas, and everyone admits that you know how to create an attractive package. But let's face it: what have you got that can stand up to the appeal of the toilet brush?

Nothing, that's what.

All the toys you've so painstakingly invented—the See and Say, the Alfie mini-computers, the battery-operated cash registers, those adorable bears that talk back, the Tiny Tears—do you know where they are right now? They're underneath kids' beds and lurking behind the refrigerator, that's where.

Remnants of them are mashed at the bottom of toy boxes, wedged behind couch cushions and smooshed under car mats. And the kids they were designed for? They're off somewhere, captivated by the turkey baster from the kitchen drawer.

Don't ask me why this is.

I spent hours roaming the toy aisles and loading up on educational, made-for-toddlers toys for Christmas, but I needn't have bothered. The stand-alone Fisher Price model kitchen, with its coffeepot, dishwasher, telephone, stove and sink, has lost the Most Fun Toy contest.

The winner, hands down, is the M-Z section of the Spanish-English dictionary.

That's what *our* 2-year-old wants to see upon awakening, and other mothers I've talked to say their kids are just as strange.

You've got to feel sorry for toy manufacturers so out of touch with consumers that they don't already know that toddlers appreciate the lid to the butter dish more than they care for all those cute little talk-back teddy bears. Where, after all, are the crackerjack teams of researchers? Are they out taking their naps?

My friend Ann can't even brush her teeth without getting a special dispensation from her 2-year-old son, because he has the family toothbrushes involved in an elaborate game. And yes, all of them are essential for this game—which seems to revolve around the toothbrushes being spirited away to distant locations and then moved again. I think it may be a Witness Protection game, actually, but Ann is less than enchanted.

"We have to beg to brush our teeth, and then he watches us carefully the whole time, and collects the toothbrushes immediately after we're finished," Ann says. "Yesterday he got suspicious because he noticed he didn't have any toothbrushes for the cats. I guess he thought we were holding out on him."

But has the Playskool company tried to market a Family Toothbrush Collection for tots? They never even dreamed of it.

Kyle, who is 1½, turned up his nose at the four-foot high basketball hoop his parents lovingly selected for him for Christmas, and instead spends day after day practicing his golf shot with the toilet brush.

We went through something similar about a year ago, when our toddler decided the toilet plunger was actually a baby doll in disguise and needed to be tucked into bed next to her each night.

I'm sure my look of horror and disgust actually made the toilet plunger more attractive to its "mommy."

But these days, the Current Favorite Object (these change rapidly, as all parents can tell you) is a four-color brochure with photographs of a line of dolls. This brochure, which cannot be purchased separately, came with a doll we bought for our daughter for Christmas.

At the time, we thought the doll herself was the real present, but that was foolish of us. She was "put to bed" in the trash can during the first week, while the brochure remains a big favorite and must be read aloud at least three times a day.

My friend Jennifer's kid will only play with an old coffee can containing two quarters and a penny. And Linda's son has taken up with a decorated Japanese chopstick he found, which he never tires of.

It's time toy manufacturers took a look around at the real world and came up with some new ideas. I think, with some help from today's toddlers, they could produce a line of toilet plungers—perhaps accessorized with pajamas, baby bottles, and layette sets—that would really turn some heads.

If not, how about some ripped-up dictionaries?

The Enemy is Dryness

My mother telephones from Florida, and just before we hang up, she always asks the same thing: "Are you moisturizing?"

"Yes," I say, rolling my eyes.

"Are you using that Super Energizing Placental Extract Hydrolyzing Cream I sent you?"

"Yes."

"And you're following it with the Eye Puffiness Minimizing Concentrate?"

"Yes."

There is a silence while she tries to decide if I'm telling the truth. Then she says, "I certainly hope you're not skipping the Eye and Throat Moisture Barrier Complex with Lanolin and Aloe."

"I would never skip that."

"Every morning and evening?"

"At least four times a day," I tell her. "I'm practically oozing the stuff. My face is so shiny that people use me as a mirror. In fact, right now I'm having to grip the telephone with both hands to keep it from sliding off my face and falling on the floor."

She is not amused.

"When you're 55 years old, and your skin looks as if a 100-year-old spider web has been fused onto it, then you'll realize I know what I'm talking about. *Then* you'll wish you'd even gone for the Vitamin E Collagen and Elastin Hydroponic Toner."

It's no wonder that my sister and I grew up thinking of moisture as a precious commodity, much like gold or silver. I was surprised when I first heard that moisture actually exists in the air, available for absolutely everybody.

For my mother—and possibly every woman of her generation—The Enemy is dryness, and it must be fought at every opportunity with expensive potions in fancy little bottles.

But I want to admit this now and be done with it: there *are* nights I go to bed without moisturizing. I know it's crazy, a woman in her 30s taking such a big chance with her skin's future.

But there are nights I am too tired, or I tell myself I already have enough moisture in my life.

There are even nights I say: so *what* if I don't have enough moisture? I am sick of thinking about moisture.

Moisture be damned, I say recklessly before I go to bed. Sometimes, in the few minutes before sleep comes, I hear my mother's voice in my head, warning me about the crinkly little lines that are forming around my eyes, etching a trough on either side of my mouth, knitting my brows together in a furrow.

But I still don't get out of bed.

My husband—a man who, near as I can tell, has never given five seconds' thought to whether he possesses enough moisture—is no help.

"You don't think this stuff works, do you?" he's prone to say. "What in the world do elastin and collagen and placental extracts have that ordinary motor oil doesn't?"

He picks up the bottles of lotion—all sent by my mother—and makes jokes about them. "Let's see, here's the Nose and Throat cream. What do you suppose would happen if some of that got on your chin? And where is the Chin Cream, or the Ear Lobe cream?"

I would have earned more of his respect, I think, if I had just chucked all those bottles in the trash can as soon as they arrived.

But I didn't.

There are times in my life when I know it's nonsensical to

fret over the lines and creases that seep onto my face, that keep up an accurate count of the laughs and smiles and frowns that perform there daily. Really, I even know there is no such thing as a moisture barrier, even if a product does claim to be Super Energizing.

But something keeps me putting the stuff on my face, almost every day. It's the idea that maybe, just maybe, the stuff is working—and if I gave up altogether, those creepy little lines would crawl all over my face.

And then my mother would draw herself up, with perfect certitude, and say, "I told you so!"

Credit Check

One of the most harrowing moments devised by our culture is the so-called Credit Check.

This is when you're standing in the checkout line of a store, with at least 25 people behind you, and the clerk looks sneeringly down at your plastic credit card and says, "Sorry, we'll have to check this."

Sometimes clerks dispense with the part about being sorry, and just snatch your card and start dialing numbers on a secret telephone stashed under the counter.

People behind you in line start to fidget and sigh. Several leave in search of a line that doesn't allow would-be embezzlers in it, and those who remain glare at you, like it's *your* fault. They must figure the store personnel recognize you from a poster shown at the last sales meeting, with DO NOT SELL ANYTHING TO THIS PERSON written above your smiling face.

Credit checks always take longer than they should.

You watch the clerk's face. Even if you know you have a $500,000 credit limit on your card, and you're totally paid up, and in fact, the bank is trying to borrow back some money from *you*, how can you possibly not watch the clerk's face to see what all those zillions of numbers mean to the person on the other end?

Surely even the Rockefellers can't be calm at a time like this.

The minutes drag on. Sometimes, of course, the clerk reads back a number and writes it down on the slip. This could be the mysterious "authorization code" or it could be the number of years they'll try to get you sent to prison for.

Worse is when there's just a long silence. Then the clerk hangs up and faces you. Either she's about to put your purchases in a bag and hand them to you, or else rip your card in two and hand you a pair of handcuffs to put on.

When I was in college, I worked at a department store, perpetrating Credit Checks on people who came in to make innocent purchases. They would hand me their cards, and I would speak the card's secrets into the telephone.

And one time the person on the other end, whose job was to listen to those numbers, whispered back: "Do you have the card in your hand? OK. Now rip it into two pieces and put it in an envelope and mail it to this address. Ready to write this down?"

I was not ready to write anything. I turned to petrified rock. The man who had handed me the card was a little larger than Andre the Giant. I didn't think he'd take kindly to watching his card being ripped up.

I handed him the phone and went on a break.

Bad as it is to be the clerk in that situation, it's worse to be the customer. One year I waited until Dec. 23 to do Christmas shopping for the children because I knew they'd search the whole house for their presents if I bought them too early.

I stood in the line at Child World, with a full cart and near-the-limit credit card. I knew it was near the limit, but I thought it might be useful to find out just how close it was.

I had forgotten how quiet a store can get while a Credit Check is being done. The people in line shifted their packages. I think someone was musing about how sad it was financial criminals are permitted to have children.

The clerk sucked in her breath in that way they have. The word was out, loud and clear: This card was a loser.

"Well, then," I said, steadying myself. "I'll just write a check. No problem."

So you think stores will trust a piece of paper when you've proven you'd willingly bilk them with a piece of plastic? The people in line snickered.

I think I did what anyone would have done. I parked the cart, went for a Coke at Wendy's, and came back an hour later to a different check-out lane and wrote a check—a perfectly good check—for all the Christmas toys.

I still cringe when they're dialing that number.

Hair Color Hell

For as long as I can remember, there are three things I've wanted in life:

1. A dishwasher that can clean pans.
2. Children who go to bed and stay there for eight hours.
3. Light brown hair with blond streaks.

These days, life being what it is, I've pretty much given up on numbers one and two, but recently I decided to make one more stab at number three.

I went to the hair salon and said to a hairstylist we'll call Bob, "Light brown hair with blond streaks, please."

Bob nodded solemnly. He looked at my hair, which was sort of light brown already but not the right kind of light brown, if you know what I mean. Then he made one of those mystifying statements that hairdressers are always uttering.

"You know, you have some ash in the lower part of your hair."

I wasn't sure what to say, so I said again, "Could I please have light brown hair with blond streaks?"

Bob looked in some books and charts and said we could "counteract the ash," whatever that meant. It sounded like a call to arms, and off we went to the hair color chair, where he painted goop on my hair and I read magazines.

The first inkling I had that we had crossed over the line into Hair Color Hell was when he was rinsing out my hair.

"Uh, how comfortable are you with a little red in your hair?" he said.

This turned out to be a euphemism for, "How would you like hair the unearthly color of a brand new fire engine, never before found in nature?"

Let me just stop here and tell you that I find it very difficult to criticize hairdressers, especially those who seem to be taking an interest in my well-being.

I actually once sat, immobile with a frozen smile, while one guy cut my hair to within a quarter-inch of its life. But this time, just as I was slumping into the chair, feeling the life force ooze out of me, I heard Bob's boss behind us.

"Bob?" he said brightly. "What exactly is our plan here?"

So Bob again got out his color charts and his books and started telling his boss about the ash in my hair and how we were counteracting it, and then his boss put his arm around Bob and they walked to the back room together and closed the door.

When Bob came out, he had some new goop, and we made jokes about my brief life as a redhead. When he rinsed the new goop out, we both nearly fell over backward because now my hair was Bozo-the-Clown Orange.

Back came the boss, wanting to know about a plan again.

This time a Hair Color Expert was called in. He said my hair had some very hot tones in it, which was nicer than saying I looked like a warning light.

"We have to cool down this hair," he said. Then the boss, Bob, and the expert all went to the back room and closed the door.

The expert came back in a few minutes and told me that hair color can always, always be fixed. He said this loudly, in case other customers were thinking of running out the door.

"This is no problem," he said. "No problem at all. Now what did you have in mind when you came in here?"

"Light brown hair, blond streaks," I said weakly. "Could we send out for a wig?"

No wig. They applied brown goop, which almost—but not quite—took away the orange. I had to leave then, because my 6-year-old needed to be picked up at day camp.

"It really looks fine," the hair people told me, and I said it back to them, just to make us all feel better.

I got to the day camp and my daughter said, "Your hair is really interesting today."

So I went back to the place the next day, and another hair color expert said she knew just what to do. She put on a different kind of goop, then streaked blond and brown into my hair—and when she got all done, I hugged her and kissed her because there was not one particle of orange or red to be seen. Just brown and blond.

As I was leaving the place, they said to me, "So! What do you do for a living?"

I felt sorry for them, I really did, but of course I had to tell them. So I smiled and said, "Well, I write a column in the newspaper about weird things that happen to me."

Thinking About Nothing

Like nearly everybody else on the planet, I have come to the conclusion that I should be taking better care of myself.

Everyone knows what *that* means.

These days, to really be taking care of yourself, you have to make your heart beat extra-fast for 20 minutes a day (snow-shoveling counts, but I don't think watching a horror movie does), and you have to eat at least two more pieces of fruit than you think you can stand every single day. (If you choose raisins, you have to eat about a billion more than you can stand.)

And then, because this is the '90s and we now know so much more about health than ever before, there's another thing you absolutely have to do: You have to meditate.

This means that you've got to sit down for a while every day and think about nothing.

Now, before I go any further, let me just stop right here and point out that this is what makes the '90s such an astonishing and refreshing decade. At almost any other period in history, if your goal was to sit down and think about nothing, people would have said all kinds of snippy things about how lazy you were.

Not today. Today, if you tell someone you meditate, they will ask you how long you can manage to think of absolutely nothing, and then it will turn out that *they* thought of *more* nothing, *more* often, and for way longer than you ever could.

Still, I am perfectly willing to do this. In fact, you will

hardly find anyone who is more delighted than I am with the idea of sitting down and thinking about nothing.

The trouble is my feet.

No sooner have I tucked them underneath me in the now-we-are-going-to-think-about-nothing position than they start to protest about how they are not getting enough blood into the toes.

Pretty soon, they are *screeching* about nerve damage so extensive that they're positive the toes are turning white and falling off. I say, "The toes are *not* going to fall off," and they say, "They are, too." And then I realize that this is not the same at all as thinking about nothing. I have not had even one nanosecond of thoughts about nothing; I have thought only about feet.

So I move them around until they stop screeching. I take long, slow, *deeeep* breaths.

This is when I notice how cold it is in the room, and how the end of my nose, particularly, is freezing. I devote a few minutes to thinking about whether it is permissible to turn up the heat during meditation, or if that would constitute thinking about *something*, and if so, would I then have to start over?

Who cares if I have to start over? Who is making the rules here, anyway? It's *cold* in here, and I can't very well concentrate on blankness if I'm freezing, can I?

I get up and turn up the heat.

Let's see: Nothing. Nothing. Nothing. Nothing.

Here's what I want to know: is the word *nothing* the same as nothing? I mean, if I just sit there and say, "Nothing," silently to myself, isn't that *really* thinking of something?

Maybe I should get up and call someone about this; you know, collect some theories from my friends, talk to some other meditators, run an informal survey, write up my findings for some yoga journal.

No, no, no. I know what this thought is. This is one of those traps they warn you about. This is what your mind does. It *wants* you to get up and do something else. You must gently lead it back to *nothingness*.

And tell it to *stay there*. Now *stay!*

Noth. Ing. Ness. Deeep breaths.

Why do you suppose Queen Elizabeth always is photographed carrying a pocketbook? What could she be carrying in there? No, really! Wouldn't you think she'd just hand it over to someone else while she gets her picture taken?

And: Why is it that when you close your eyes, you see all these little colors flitting around in front of you? Which is better, paper or plastic? How did JFK get Marilyn Monroe smuggled into the White House? Why is it that if you think too hard about swallowing, it gets harder to do it? And do other people dust the tops of their door frames?

I peek open one eye. Five minutes have passed.

Five minutes! My head feels light.

I don't know how much more good care of myself I can stand. I'll have to eat some raisins and think about it.

The First Stages Of Dementia

Homeless Objects

I never wanted to admit that there were homeless objects right in my own home.

I was ashamed. I had been raised to believe that everything had a place, and that it was my Chief Role in Life to find that place and remember where it was.

Spoons? Right-hand kitchen drawer. Towels? Bathroom closet, second shelf. Garden hose? Basement floor, curled in a circle.

But it didn't take me very long in life to discover that a fair number of objects were hostile to the idea of being put in a category. They were unwilling to be known as spoons, or towels, or garden hoses.

They had no places I could think of.

Like the cassette tape I made when I was 10 years old, in which I pretended to be a disk jockey from Mars interviewing the earthlings in my house. Just where, I ask you, is *that* supposed to go?

I'll tell you where it *did* go: the kitchen junk drawer, where it falls out every time I need a screwdriver. I have moved this cassette tape through my last 13 moves without ever once listening to it.

But obviously it can't be thrown away; it can't be put with similar objects, because there are no similar objects, and so I am forced to run into it at least once a week. I can find it more easily than I can locate my house keys half the time.

My friend Alice is the one who made me realize I could

come out of the closet on this issue, if you'll pardon the expression. She is one of the most organized women in America, having learned the uses of a manila folder early in life. She knows and can tell you in one second who she owes letters to, who owes letters to her, and when her car was last serviced.

But she has this picture on her desk that has defeated her.

It's just a picture of a tree—a nondescript, everyday tree—but what stops her from throwing it out is the date scrawled on the back: October 1950.

No one knows where this picture came from, but ever since it fell out of the world onto Alice's desk, she has had to move it from spot to spot. It can't be thrown away; it's Old and Therefore Possibly Valuable. And it certainly doesn't belong in the album with the family pictures.

But my friend Lisa has perhaps the worst case of Object Limbo I've ever heard of. She has two daughters who are constantly out-growing their clothes, and right now she's waiting for the little one to grow into a pair of the older one's jeans.

"Now what do you think I should do with the jeans while we wait for them to fit Sarah?" she asked me.

How should I know?

Lisa's solution has been to put the jeans through the laundry again and again. These jeans actually *live* in transit from the laundry basket to the washing machine and dryer. There will surely be nothing left of them by the time Sarah can fit into them.

But what can you do with old ALF lunch boxes? Come on, we all know there's not a child in the whole country who would still take one to school, and we also know these are objects designed not to wear out. Why, a school bus could roll over one of these lunch boxes and the crunchy peanut butter in the sandwich wouldn't even turn to creamy.

I personally have a collection of ALF, Care Bear, My Little Pony, and Strawberry Shortcake lunch boxes crammed into the cabinet where I keep the baking tins. Periodically I move them to the closet where the brooms hang, but they're a nuisance there too, so they get stacked up next to the usually un-employed turkey roasting pan, where Thanksgiving morning I say, "What? These things again?"

Or how about the brochure from the place we stayed in Cape Cod last year? I can't throw it away, because someone might ask me, "Where was that place that the hurricane nearly knocked down, and your kids threw up all over?" and then I wouldn't be able to remember the name.

So this brochure just floats through the house, settling for a while on the pile of bills, then transferring itself to the letters-we-really-mean-to-answer pile, occasionally darting upstairs to rest on the headboard of our bed. Yesterday I found it on the pancakes page of the "Joy of Cooking" cookbook.

It's just one of those objects that stays on permanent tour. It's one of the adventurous guys, refusing the button-down life that a spoon opts for every time.

The Art of
Message-Mangling

This is to my friend John, whoever you may be: I probably won't be returning your call anytime soon.

You, I'm afraid, were the innocent victim of a child taking a telephone message.

As happens so often in our family, I heard of your attempt at telephonic communication from our three-year-old, who was prancing around the dinner table.

Suddenly she stopped, mid-prance. "Oh. Your friend John called you today," she said. "He wants you to call him back."

"John who?" I said.

She frowned. "Oh, I don't know *that*. But he told me his phone number." Then she laughed. "I think he thought I could write!"

The whole family—including the two older children, who have garbled messages for years—laughed uproariously.

And then we all started trying to figure out who John could be.

Did he have a deep voice? Did he know your name? Did he say if he was at home or at his office? Did he say he'd call again?

She pondered each question for quite some time, but nothing came to mind.

Later—long after bedtime—she came downstairs and said, "I just remembered part of his phone number."

"Great," I said. "What is it?"

"Zero."

You can imagine how pleased I was.

Actually, I'd say she's well on her way to becoming an expert in the art of Message-Mangling, which I expect someday to see as an Olympic sport for children. Who knows? Before she reaches her adulthood, she might make it into the Messed-Up-Message Hall of Fame.

After all these years, I think I've finally figured out just what the rules are that children live by when they are giving phone messages to their parents. It may seem like a haphazard system, but there's actually a very clear etiquette at work.

Here are the basic tenets:

1. Don't give any message before it is time. You *never* want to blurt out a message when your parent first arrives home. Best to be cool and give the message the third or fourth time you happen to think of it.

2. Be sure you know what a message actually *is*. If a person calls and leaves his name but *doesn't* speak the magic words "Tell her I called" or "Please ask her to get back to me," then you have no responsibilities whatsoever.

3. If you write a message on paper, you are not required to deliver it in person. (This may go without saying.) There is no excuse for delivering a message twice. Don't waste your breath telling your parents something they could find on their own, if only they knew where to look.

4. Don't bother looking for a decent slip of paper to write a message on. Use whatever is handy: the back of the phone book, the bottom of your shoe, a dinner napkin you find in the trash can.

5. Abbreviate, abbreviate, abbreviate. This isn't *school*, for heaven's sake. Write the message as fast as you can, with any shorthand method you can invent on the spot—and go away, feeling good that you've done your part.

Before her kids grew up and acquired lives that required responsible message-taking, my friend Alice came home nearly daily to find this kind of thing written on the blackboard next to her phone: "G C—C T D Th O F."

Any fool would know it means: "Grandma called. Come to dinner on Thursday or Friday."

More challenging was the time she came home to find on the blackboard a message that simply said: "Diane Greek Queens 30 called." This was a real stumper, and the child who had scrawled this mysterious sentence was off camping with friends for the weekend.

Alice rounded up everyone she knew to think of its possible meanings. My job was to flip through mythology textbooks to come up with names of Greek queens, especially ones who might have reigned around 30 B.C.

Nothing clicked.

Eventually it turned out that the message had been left by a woman named Diane, whom Alice hadn't talked to for 30 years, when they had both been students in a Greek class at Queens College.

Sometimes, in order to understand a kid's message-taking system, you have to be willing to review your whole life.

I've actually spent hours thinking up every acquaintance named John I've known since junior high school, but so far I can't imagine any of them calling.

Or me calling John. After all, I don't have much to go on here. Just a zero.

An Organized Person

As soon as it's officially September, I am turning my life around.

I will be an Organized Person.

You know the type. You see them in the grocery store with their coupon books, searching the shelves for the product that will save them 35 cents. I have to admit this now: Never in my life have I managed to get a coupon to the grocery store.

In fact, I can't understand how people *ever* get coupons to the grocery store.

If I run across a useful coupon in a magazine, what are the chances the scissors would happen to be within reach? Zero. So I would get up and go to the pencil cup beside the telephone, where the orange-handled scissors are supposed to hang out, but when I got to the phone, no doubt I would remember that I was supposed to make a doctor's appointment for one of the kids, and I would do that, only I'd have to stop a minute to find a pen to write the time on the calendar.

That would lead me to rummaging through the kitchen drawers, where I'd be likely to find those beads I meant to restring (why not now?) or a recipe for enchiladas I could make—but only if I went *that minute* to the store for sour cream.

By the time I'd bought the sour cream, repaired the beads, found a pen, called the doctor's office and written the appointment on the calendar, I'd be so impressed with myself for accomplishing five hard things that I'd put aside my search for the scissors (which are *never* in the pencil cup), and weeks later I'd come across the magazine under the couch and say, "What is this old magazine hanging around for?" and toss it out.

At least that's the old me.

The New Me, reborn every September—pulling herself from the wreckage of an idle and foolish summer and marching forward to meet a glorious and productive autumn—is always going to know where the scissors are, which magazines have coupons, and what we are having for dinner every night at least 30 minutes before I begin to cook it.

And since it's September, and I'm at the height of my organizational powers, I'm even going to do the task that's so enormous that I've put it off for a whole year.

You see, a friend moved away and left 75 phonograph albums in our attic. Over the past year, we have gone from the joking, "Ha Ha, maybe you could mail those records to me one of these months" to the openly hostile, "Surely even *you* could have found a moment to mail those records!"

A moment! Who is he kidding? Mailing these records involves at least 14 steps. First of all, I'd have to look for boxes that are strong enough to support records. I don't even know if such boxes exist. But assuming I found some, I'd then have to find and buy heavy-duty packing tape. And plastic foam peanuts— does anybody know where they come from? As far as I know, you have to get them in the mail from somebody else's boxes.

Then I'd have to put all the records into the boxes. The boxes would have to be wrapped in brown paper (where are those scissors?) and a label attached. I'd have to look up the address, call my friend to get the ZIP code, and tie the whole thing with string.

And I didn't even get to the post office yet.

Days that require a trip to the post office are nearly impossible. There is never a place to park. Then I have to figure out how to get those heavy boxes inside. And find the correct line. Probably I'd realize I should have stopped at a cash machine on the way, so I could finance this venture.

I'm only willing to consider this project because it's September, and this is the kind of heroic act I'm up for. Just yesterday I dragged the records out and started sorting through them.

Hey, I thought, before I mail these, I should really transfer some of them to tape. I might need these songs for my personal collection.

This has set things back a bit because now I need to buy some cassette tapes. And I know that, in a magazine I saw just last month, there was a coupon for cassettes.

I'm going to drop everything today and start looking for that magazine—and the scissors— and get this done. I promise.

Losing My Mind

This is going to be a sad story about a woman systematically losing her mind. If you are feeling gloomy already, or do not know where your house keys are, I would suggest you move along quietly.

This is the story of how I have gone mad searching for my keys over the course of an entire day.

Even while I am writing this, I am *still* obsessively searching for these keys. I keep jumping up to look in yet one more place. Are they perhaps under the keyboard to the word processor? In the desk drawer? Behind the bookcase?

No, they are not.

Neither are they in any of the three bags of gooey garbage I have gone through twice (I may have to go through them a third time before I can find true peace), or between the couch cushions, or hanging on the Christmas tree. Other places they are not: in the baby's diaper pail, the cat's food dish, or on top of the refrigerator. And obviously, they are not in my purse nor in my coat pocket.

Now that it's been a full 24 hours since the search began, family members have begun to back away when they see me coming. I suspect that it's my "looking for lost object" expression that has frightened them.

Periodically I shout at them: "Would one of you *puh-lease* look in the dishwasher once more?" It gets tiresome being the only one to think of places that need rechecking.

It has been patiently explained to me several times that my

keys have no reason to be in the dishwasher. Frankly, I am tired of that kind of logic. Can't people understand that we're now in a special warp of the universe, and none of the old rules applies?

"Where did you last see them?" these people keep asking me, as if that has any relation to where the keys now are. If I weren't standing on the refrigerator, checking the cabinet where I keep the turkey roasting pan, I would clobber the person asking me that question *again*.

Instead, I calmly tell the story. It was two days ago, and I was coming into the house with a load of groceries in one arm and a sleeping 17 pound baby precariously in the other. I handed the keys to my 9-year-old daughter, who distinctly remembers balancing her bag of groceries against her knees while she opened the door.

The rest is a blur. The two bags of groceries and the baby made it into the house, but the keys took advantage of the momentary confusion to escape forever.

Whenever I get to this point in the story, I leap up and run to check the lock again. But the keys still are not there.

The 9-year-old is understandably a bit more frightened than the rest of the family because she senses she has a major role in this production. Her head hurts, she says, from thinking so much about what she did after she unlocked the front door.

She takes one look at my face and volunteers to look in the dishwasher one more time. "Good idea," I tell her.

Later she says she's going to spend her allowance to buy me one of those keychains that beeps whenever you clap your hands in a certain way. I had one of those once, and it was exhilarating to be in constant communication with my keys. I never had to go looking for them, because the keys were always beeping away, like a friendly reassurance: "Here I am! Over here!"

I had to disconnect it, though, in a movie theater, when an usher politely requested that I immediately shut off whatever was making that hideously disturbing noise, or both it and I would be out the door. The key beeper never got over the shock of being silenced and refused to work ever again.

By that time, I was actually just as pleased to be without it, because it had gotten slightly embarrassing to advertise to the whole world that I was the kind of moron who couldn't keep keys without a tracking device.

And so, consequently, here I am slipping into the first stages of dementia. I can't even remember what I used to do before I spent all my time looking through garbage cans and behind cushions.

Tomorrow I'm resolving to have a new set of keys made. First, though, I'm planning to get up in the middle of the night and snatch open the silverware drawer. I have a hunch that at night, the keys go in there to frolic around with the spoons.

The Object Relocation Program

I wouldn't dream of leaving home without alerting my 5-year-old daughter first.

Actually, I can't. Only she knows where my car keys are.

Most likely, she's also in possession of my hat, my gloves, and any number of objects from my purse.

And it's not as if I could look around and simply find all these things on my own. She most likely has trotted them off to some mysterious, unthinkable location: perhaps to be of some use to the baby dolls whom she forces to live behind the television set, or to keep company with the videotapes she has underneath the kitchen sink, or even to be vacationing with the Legos in that space between her bike tires and the wall of the garage.

It would take trained hound dogs hours to find all my things.

"Why? Why? Why?" I said to her the other day, after a hysterical 15-minute search. "Why is my wallet living behind the bag of charcoal on the back porch?"

She gazed at me coolly. "Your wallet, if you didn't realize it, is a sleeping bag for Barbie's baby."

"But why does Barbie's baby need *my wallet* to be a sleeping bag?"

"Barbie is the kind of mother who likes to take her babies camping, and she wants them to be comfortable."

That's the kind of answer I always get.

I was about to say, "Then let Barbie go out and buy her babies sleeping bags," but then I realized Barbie would no doubt still require my wallet.

This, incidentally, is a long-standing problem between me and my 5-year-old. I suspect I gave birth to an Object Relocator, and that there is no known cure.

In the delivery room, in fact, when she looked around at the world with her filmy newborn gaze, I now know she was scanning for objects she could smuggle out of there when they took her to the nursery. Perhaps she thought all that fetal monitoring equipment really should be moved to the hospital cafeteria.

And all that crying she did in her crib? It's now obvious to me she wanted to reach up and rip out that Winnie-the-Pooh mobile we'd hung for her amusement. No doubt she had in mind just the perfect spot for it, in the bathroom behind the box of baby wipes.

From the time she could walk, no item was safe in its designated spot. She cruised through the house with a toy shopping cart, and just like a purchaser browsing through a department store, she casually picked up items and took them elsewhere. I'd come upon all the serving spoons tucked away in her sock drawer. Her pajamas turned up underneath the ironing board in the linen closet. The bag of cat food somehow was destined to live in the dryer.

While other people's babies were stacking up the kitchen chairs so they could reach the cookie jar above the refrigerator, mine was nonchalantly stashing my paycheck in that crack between the radiator and the bathroom wall.

Oh, it's been a long, long 5½ years. But we've made it.

And now, as she explains to me, in her All Grown Up Style—hands on hips, hair turned under just so, pink satin purse slung over her shoulder—"You don't have to always get so crazy when you can't find things. All you have to do is ask me. I do know where everything is, you know."

And she does.

"The pancake syrup?" I ask.

Mrs. Butterworth has been sent down to the playroom, where she's babysitting Barbie's baby—— the one who had to leave her campsite in the middle of the night, after her sleeping bag was so rudely taken away from her.

"Your brother's calculator that he needs for school?"

Ah. That's under her pillow, where she was attempting to calculate how old she has to be before we finally realize she's all grown up.

I want to pull her onto my lap and tell her that's still a long time away. I don't, because that's not what she wants to hear, and it's probably not true anyway.

But I begin to see, just a little bit, the root of the Object Relocation Program. If we all have to ask her where everything is, then that's a little bit of power she has that no one can dispute.

So, instead, I say to her, "Do you have any idea where my house keys are?"

And she smiles and says, "Of course! I put them in Daddy's coat pocket right before he left for work."

A Separate
Climate Zone

The Soundtrack of Winter

When I moved to the Northeast from California 15 years ago, my Uncle Bob (a man who had seen true winters) had only one piece of advice: "Keep the heat turned up high enough so you can still drink iced tea."

My Uncle Bob, as you can see, knew how to live the good life.

Naturally, with a philosophy that sound, he knew enough to help us unpack just a few boxes and then hightail it back to California. I've been stuck here ever since, trying to figure out where I'd get the piles of money needed to follow his advice.

I must tell you now that there are days in my very own house when I cannot drink a glass of iced tea unless I'm in the bathtub, and it's filled to the brim with hot water. One lousy glass of iced tea, and it somehow requires the *entire* contents of the hot water heater.

But I expected this.

I knew New England would be cold. They told us all about it in geography class back in fourth grade.

What they *didn't* tell us was the True Story of Household Heat. Perhaps they thought we weren't strong enough to take it. They explained snow, sleet, and ice over and over again, but not once did a teacher think to say, "By the way, if you ever move to New England, don't get the kind of house where you will buy thousands of dollars worth of heat that will go directly into your kitties and bypass your whole house."

If anyone had bothered to tell me that, chances are I would have never moved into a house that had heating vents built into the floor. Convenient, cat-sized heating vents, one for each of our kitties.

For two whole winters, we came home every day, only to find icicles growing from the ceiling—while the cats stretched luxuriously across the vents. These kitties were so pumped up with our fuel oil dollars, they were actually too hot to touch.

We were pretty pleased with ourselves the day we moved to a house with a sensible system like radiators. I saw them as rather friendly devices that wouldn't put up with ice formations indoors, yet didn't have aspirations of becoming comfy armchairs either.

Functional, I thought. No nonsense. You could tell by looking at them that they were designed for Important Heating Responsibilities.

That was before I knew radiators actually have their own agendas.

Right now as I write this, all the radiators in this house are *screaming*. I don't know if they are screaming at us, or if there is merely some radiator imbroglio going on.

All I know is that the kitchen radiator is now shrieking as if it belonged in the kind of horror movie where no one ends up alive. Upstairs, it's being answered cheerfully—or maybe even taunted—by one of the bedroom radiators which is bumping along like popcorn in a hot pan, saying, "Bobba-da-bobba-da-bobba-da." Nice beat. You could dance to that radiator.

Howling from the living room and dining room are the Tiger Fight Radiators, dueling systems that trade screeches like two wild tigers scratching each other's eyes out. They can growl and cry back and forth unceasingly, and never get their problems worked out.

For sheer hostility, though, you can't beat our downstairs bathroom radiator, which hisses ominously at you for hours on end, and then if you fail to be frightened away, lets loose with a drenching cloud of steam. I have seen my children running out of the bathroom, looking over their shoulders in panic.

The radiator in our bedroom, though, is my favorite for sheer showmanship. It seems to think of itself as a gong left over from the Chinese New Year, responsible for keeping up a constant clanging and banging all winter long. At 6 a.m. in our bedroom, you would think all the pots and pans were being beaten with baseball bats.

What amazes me is that I've come to think of this as merely the soundtrack of winter—nothing worth even interrupting a conversation for.

I hadn't thought how weird it all was for years. But recently, a little boy came to visit us from California. As soon as the Tiger Fight Radiators started up, he got his coat and went outside.

"I can't stay in there," he said. "You seem to have a dragon loose somewhere in your house."

And all this time I thought they were tigers.

A Christmas Mistake

Year after year, without exception, I forget the real meaning of the Christmas vacation from school: it's a time for parents to be transformed from their humdrum selves and shown their Real Purpose in Life—to be some kid's audience.

I just came off of 10 days of being some kid's audience—my 4-year-old daughter Stephanie's— and it had gotten to the point where I didn't have any of my natural responses anymore.

Say something to me, and I automatically started clapping.

Sing something to me, and I started jumping up and down, shouting, "Hurray! Hurray!"

What's worse, I have to admit, is that I brought it on myself.

I was performing that famous holiday ritual, known as Last Minute Shopping for the Kids—you know, living through those panicky moments on Dec. 24, when the stores are all about to close and you know Christmas won't be complete without just *one more present* for everybody—and I snatched up, through the rubble of the toy department, an actual, electronic children's guitar.

My husband frowned. Something must have stirred in his over-holidayed brain cells that knew this wasn't the best idea I'd ever had.

But I was insistent. "It's only a *toy* guitar," I said. "You know how musical she seems to be. She'll spend hours off by herself practicing songs."

Only later—Christmas afternoon, to be exact—did I discover that even toy guitars these days come with amplifiers and microphones, and have the ability to produce that excruciating noise known as feedback.

And later I discovered something even worse.

Apparently you can't play a guitar with amplifiers and microphones and wonderfully screeching feedback without adopting a new persona to go with the experience. There's no such thing as taking an amplified guitar off by yourself and just strumming a few notes in your aloneness.

No. When you have *this* kind of guitar (and I really do think there should have been a warning on the box), you have to put on glittery dress-up clothes, sunglasses—and anywhere you go, you have to *burst* into the room, strumming some wildness with you as you go.

"LADIES AND GENTLEMEN, I am the most beautiful and famous girl singer there ever was"—strum, strum, strum, screech of feedback—"The incredible MISS COMMANDA!"

Apparently that's what you have to say. And your parents are supposed to look not only impressed, but *grateful* that they have in their midst such an unbelievable presence. They are supposed to drop what they are doing *immediately*, as if, say, the Beatles or New Kids on the Block had just twanged their way into the room.

I must admit, I am found wanting.

I can only sit, untwitching, for 10 or 15 minutes, listening to the stream-of-consciousness songs. They all go something like this one:

"The children had their dinner,
And the Christmas lights were on,
And the tablecloth had a spot on it,
But no one cared because they wanted to go to
    Burger King anyway.
She wanted crackers,
Oh, she wanted crackers,
But I said no, the doll is hungry too.
So they went to Burger King.

Now my mommy is leaving the room—
HEY! COME BACK! I'M NOT FINISHED!"

But I tell Miss Commanda that I have pots boiling over on the stove, or that the telephone is ringing—anything to buy a little time. And then, feeling guilty, I slink back later and listen to the rest of the show, which often features Barney and all the baby dolls she got for Christmas.

Silently I count the days before nursery school begins again.

Last year, the Mistake Present of the Season was a restaurant set. Because of it, she became, *overnight*, the waitress from hell, who woke us up at the crack of dawn each morning, standing there with pencil and notepad, asking, "What your whole lunch is?"

As time wore on and the line between reality and diner life became more blurry, she took to asking, "What your whole life is?"

I wish she'd ask me that again. Now I know what my whole life is. It's to be an audience.

See? I'm clapping, I'm clapping.

The Driveway

I meant not to complain about my driveway. When winter started—way back in October or November, I believe—and those heavy white flakes started coming down faster and faster, I made a pact with myself. I said: I will not write about my driveway.

I said: I will shovel the thing and keep quiet about it.

Besides, there wasn't going to be any need to think about the driveway. Last summer, when my husband's parents visited, they brought with them a snow blower. They had bought a Huge Super Deluxe Snow-blower for themselves, the kind that can eat up all the snow in the Midwest in one hungry gulp, and so they were giving us their moderate-sized one.

It was July, and the thing looked cartoonish out there in the 90-degree heat—with its huge black snow-eating teeth and all. My husband and I did a high-five. No more driveway problems this year! Or ever!

It is now nearly March, it has been over 50 degrees for days now, and I would just like to say that our driveway still has *lots* of snow on it. We have green grass and earthworms in the back yard, but one could still construct a giant snowman in the driveway.

This confirms what I have suspected since we moved here two years ago: The driveway is in its own separate climate zone.

I'm sure it will turn out that, due to some freak geological formations or the erratic way the glaciers receded back in the

Ice Age, our driveway is actually a portion of Greenland that got left behind by accident.

Luckily I have joined an informal Displaced-From-Greenland Driveway Support Group this winter. It's a telephone group, of course. It has to be. When you need the meetings the most, you can't get out to attend them.

In fact, the Support Group has most of its meetings while the whole rest of the world is happily out leading its regular life. The sun is shining, streets are plowed, even schools are in session—but when you've got a displaced driveway, none of that matters.

You are stuck at home.

These days, when my friend Mary calls to see how things are going, she doesn't start with, "How are you?" She says, "How's the driveway?"

She wants details, too. Not like some people who just want you to say, "fine," and if you really try to tell them how the driveway is, they start sighing and rolling their eyes.

With Mary, I can say, "Well, the lower 10 feet has the kind of crusty ice that's going to take about five pounds of rock-salt, but up near the pine trees there's just loose snow."

"How's the center section where the turn is?" she wants to know.

So then I tell her how the snow blower balked at getting rid of all the snow in the center section, and then Mary tells me that the same thing happened in *her* driveway.

"It seems like the kind of snow that the snow blower just spits back out," she says.

"Yes!" I say. "And then it leaves behind this very slippery coating . . . "

"And then you have to get the shovel and really work at scraping it up," she adds.

"I had to actually go for the ice hoe," I tell her.

"The ice hoe! I didn't think of that. I just used the hard-edged shovel when the scooper shovel didn't work."

"Try the ice hoe and *then* the scooper," I say. "Then, later, you can go over the whole thing once more with the regular hard-edged shovel."

Later, my friend Jane calls to say that she'd gotten the snow almost all cleaned up, but then it got 10 degrees colder, and everything that had melted froze again, and so now she fears black ice on the driveway.

Black Ice.

There's a moment of silence. In the Support Group, black ice is much feared: You get a black ice situation going, and you may never get out.

"I was using just plain dirt, and then I went to Kitty Litter, but now I think I'm going to have to use up the rest of the rock salt," she says.

"I think you should call Mary and Jennifer and Elaine and see what they think," I say.

And after that, I think we should get Greenland on the phone and say there are some driveways out here they need to retrieve.

A Snow Day

I know that what I feel is not legally classifiable as cabin fever until I'm stuck inside for at least another 72 hours—but I think I qualify for an early diagnosis on account of being inside for a whole day with a 5-year-old.

Oh, stop yelling at me. I'm aware of the fact that lots of people stay inside for days on end with 5-year-olds. I know there are people in this world who actually *teach* 5-year-olds and spend endless hours with hordes of them every day.

But this was not just any 5-year-old.

This was a 5-year-old under the influence of the video "Aladdin."

This was a 5-year-old who thinks she lives in the Middle East, and that the only reason the rest of us are on the planet is so we can serve as the extras in her own little Aladdin movie.

I should have seen this coming. A week ago I took her to Friendly's for dinner, and when the waitress said hello to us, Stephanie yelled out, "Salaam and good evening!"

Most people might not know that those are the opening lines of "Aladdin." I didn't know it myself at the time. But then came the Snow Day.

Stephanie thought this was a Watch Aladdin All Day Long Day.

When told that she wouldn't have to go to school, she leaped into the air and screamed, "Ten thousand years can really give you a crick in the neck! Boy, it's good to be out of there!"

This didn't make much sense to me, so, like any mother with 127 inches of unshoveled icy snow in her driveway, I ignored it.

But then she came over to me, eyes narrowed, talking in a New York accent: "Are you lookin' at me? Did you rub my lamp? Did you bring me here, and now you're walkin' out on me? I don't *think* so!"

"Help!" I screamed.

"Calm down, she's just doing Robin Williams, playing the part of the genie in 'Aladdin,' " said my husband.

I came back in the room. "What would you like to do today?" I said to her. "Want to bake cookies?"

"I want to watch 'Aladdin,' " she said.

We watched it. I was the kind of audience that sat on the couch and looked at the TV set. She was the kind of audience that ran around the room shouting the lines a half-second before the cartoon characters did.

At the end, I was forced to sing Aladdin's part in "A Whole New World," which meant rewinding the tape over and over again until I got the lines just right.

"Now let's go sledding," I said.

"I don't want to, because I'll have to change out of my Aladdin pajamas," she said.

"But you can wear your Aladdin sweatshirt and Aladdin socks! That'll be two Aladdin items instead of just one."

"But the pajamas have a bigger picture of the princess."

"Forget the princess and come outside."

We went into the frozen world outside. The snow crunched under our boots as we dragged the sleds up the hill. The world felt silent, and so cold we were almost breathless.

I tucked her inside the sled and got in behind her. "This is my favorite hill," I said. "Hold on tight."

She smiled up at me. "Keep your hands and arms inside the magic carpet. Please remain seated until the carpet comes to a complete stop. The emergency exits are located here, here, here, here and here."

We flew down the hill and glided to a stop next to a tree.

"Thank you for flying Magic Carpet Airlines. Thank you and watch your step," she said.

"I don't know if I'm going to make it," I said to my husband later. "I'm starting to miss living with a sane person."

When we went inside, she wanted to watch you-know-what again, but I held firm.

"We're already in the danger zone with that movie," I told her.

She glared at me. "Am I sultan or am I sultan?"

We had to call a moratorium, I'm afraid. But that night, before she fell asleep, she asked, pitifully, "Could I just say a few lines to help myself go to sleep?"

"Sure," I said.

I sat there while she did half the movie, in funny voices. When she finally wound down, she said, "Tomorrow, if it's still snowy, let's do the magic carpet again."

I'm praying for an early spring.

Winter's Enchantment

It's time I came clean about something: I secretly love the winter.

OK, not the roads. No one could love the roads.

And maybe not quite so many school closings.

But certainly everything else about it: the snow, the icicles, the cold, and of course, the brand-new conversations you get to have with your friends.

Take the Blizzard of '78, for instance. I have lots of friends now whom I didn't know during the Blizzard of '78, and so it's a relief to finally get to hear how *they* spent that blizzard, how many miles they had to walk in the blowing snow, how many days they remained in their houses before their first homicidal impulses toward family members, and precisely what item it was that they could no longer live without, causing them to hurtle themselves out the door through the blinding snowfall.

In my case, it was diapers.

You see? Some of my newer friends are just learning this about me, and I think it's safe to say this completes their full understanding of my situation back in 1978, when I was the mother of an 18-month-old.

Believe me, these fascinating what-did-you-do-during-the-'78 blizzard conversations are quickly replacing the where-were-you-during-the-Kennedy-assassination conversations that used to be so satisfying. These days, what with so many people growing up and all, you can run into quite a few otherwise intelligent people who didn't even bother to get *born* before the JFK incident, and so they really don't have much to say about their whereabouts that day.

Thank God we still have blizzards to connect us to each other.

And speaking of connecting, only a winter like this could have led me to discover an amazing fact about teen-agers: they *will* shovel snow, but only if you call it "weight-lifting" instead of snow shoveling, and if you don't mind that the lifting gets done in the middle of the night.

My son has gotten so enthusiastic about his new midnight "weight-lifting" regime that he's not only shoveled our impossible driveway every night, but has also shoveled a path through the entire length of the back yard for the dog's bathroom purposes.

Few homeowners I know have a shoveled back yard.

There's another advantage to winter that simply must not be overlooked.

It's the Cancellation Factor.

In a winter like this, you can almost always count on the fact that anything you really don't want to do is going to be canceled anyway.

We've certainly seen this work well for schoolchildren, but it can work for adults, too.

Go ahead: schedule yourself for boring committee meetings, dentist appointments, ingrown toenail treatments. Most likely you'll never have to go because some storm or other will be sweeping into the area just as it's time to get in the car.

But even if no storm arrives precisely at the right time, the great thing about winter is that you can always claim that your driveway is too slippery to get down, or that you're still plowed in from the *last* major snowstorm. Then, after you've made your excuse, just quickly turn the topic over to what you were doing in the Blizzard of '78 and how much better or worse that situation was for you—and I think you've gotten yourself clear of any further obligations.

The other good news about winter is that it's truly one of

the greatest seasons, dog-wise. My dog, who is a little misguided in his notion of what constitutes Useful Dog Work (he thinks we'll be pleased when he wrestles to the ground and then rips apart the kitchen sponge, for instance), considers it his duty to personally *eat* as much snow as he can.

Since winter began, I believe he has rid our driveway of probably three entire tablespoons of snow.

This has given him a whole new purpose in life, other than barking at mail deliverers and harassing our sponges. When he and the kids come in from their various snow-removal exercises, they're totally wiped out.

In fact, they're so tired that all they can do is lie there while I tell them lots of fascinating stories about my life. I tell them all about what I was doing on the day Kennedy was shot—and if I'm lucky, before their eyes completely close, I detail for them once again how hard the snow was coming down in the Blizzard of '78.

I also tell the dog I'm sure he could have eaten practically a whole driveway's worth of snow then.

February

My friend Elsa called me with bad news.

She's breaking up with her boyfriend because twice in one week he has forgotten to ask her how her work is going.

Twice in one week.

"Elsa," I said. "It's February. Give the guy a break."

But this was twice in one week. And add that to the fact that Elsa gained five pounds over the holidays, and his response when she happened to mention this disgusting fact to him. Did he say, "Oh, but you still look wonderful to me"? No, he did not. He, in fact, said, "Well, I guess we both could stand to cut back a little at the feed bag."

The *feed bag*, said Elsa. Now just what kind of a man would say a phrase like "feed bag" to a woman he supposedly loves, and right near Valentine's Day too?

"Repeat after me," I said. "It's February, Feb. Ru. Ar. Y."

Elsa, it turns out, hates people who pronounce the "ru" in February. Where she grew up, they say Feb-yoo-ary.

Do you see what I mean? February is a dangerous month. There must be a reason they don't let it have a full 30 or 31 days. February is so bad it had to be limited by legislation to a mere 28 days, and I guess everybody knows why: Nobody can stay sane all the way through. The whole world is too cold, too difficult, and just too much trouble.

My 16-year-old son just ambled into the room, a look of vague dissatisfaction on his face. I knew that look immediately.

"Be careful," I told him. "Anything you say to me right now is going in the column."

But even that warning couldn't keep him quiet. He leaned against my desk, folded his arms, and had a revelation. He has figured out, he said, that everything he's now doing and everything he's *supposed* to be doing but is *not* doing—all of this is *my* fault.

"Why is this my fault?" I said, fingers poised on the keys.

"You try to do too many things. You've always got a million things going on, so I do that too, and then I can't finish everything, and I get too stressed out," he said. "You know deep down that I wouldn't try to do so many things if I didn't see you doing it. Admit it."

"Thank you," I said. "You've just proven what I've been saying about February."

He swiped the bottle of hand cream and a tube of Chapstick off my dresser before leaving. "Why isn't this stuff ever in my room, where I need it?" he muttered. "And why does February have two 'R's in it anyway? Nobody ever pronounces it right."

And I had such high hopes for this winter, too.

This was the winter I was going to be cheerful all the way through. I was going to pace myself like athletes do—not even let myself think about the lack of warm weather until at least late April, and even the worst I'd say then would be, "Well, spring has got to get here sometime, ha ha ha."

I was going to strive for the kind of winter where I basked in appreciation of the small things: the way the kitchen windows steam up when you make soup; the leafy pattern that ice makes on the windshield; even that delightful howling sound the wind makes as it scrapes the branches against our house.

Sleet? Snow? Bring them on! I'd find something good about all types of weather this year!

But I've got to admit it now; I can't take much more. It's all too much.

My car doors are frozen shut, and I can only get in by crawling through the hatch.

My lips are so chapped they're sharper than my teeth.

Two of my three children are home from school, spreading the famous Headache-Stomachache Virus all over the household surfaces. This is the necessary follow-up to the Sneezing-Coughing Virus they spread around last week.

The pockets are ripped in my winter coat, the left index finger on my best pair of gloves has started to unravel, and the heel broke on one of my gray boots.

And guess what? Elsa called back. Her pipes burst, her car battery died between errands while she was downtown, and three people sneezed on her in line at the bank.

But the good news: She's delaying the breakup with her boyfriend because he sent over some flowers for Valentine's Day with a card that said, "So how was your day?"

It's February, I told her. Be careful out there.

Monsters of
Convenience

A Cash-Machine Horror Story

It's time to take a moment out from appreciating springtime to give thanks for our monsters of convenience—cash-machine cards.

Oh, don't start yelling. I know as well as anyone that cash-machine cards are probably single-handedly responsible for most of the problems in society.

It's obvious that without bank cards, some people would probably have an approximate idea of how much money they have in their bank accounts, and a few of us might even still retain the dream of someday agreeing with the bank on just what that amount is.

And I'm sure I don't have to tell you how many trees would've been saved if cash machines didn't generate thousands of pieces of paper with each transaction.

But we have to be fair here. There's an up side to cash-machine cards, too, besides the fact that they make it possible for you to draw out all your money and impulsively spend it on things you'll later wish you'd never seen.

Cash-machine cards bring people together.

I was at a cash machine the other day, having made the impulsive decision to pay off in cash my skyrocketing Children's Allowance debt rather than trying to convince the children to accept MasterCard.

The line was long, so I had plenty of time to stand there fidgeting with the rest of the cash-starved population. As I al-

ways do when I'm stuck in cash-machine lines, I tried to figure out where you're supposed to look.

The unspoken etiquette requires that you *not* try to peer
over the machine users' shoulders and figure out their secret
codes. That much I know. But why is it that everyone in a
cash line is required to stare down at the floor, in complete silence?

The man communing with the machine was pushing buttons like mad and periodically groaning, so I had plenty of
time to muse on Line-Standing Behavior of Bank Card
Users.

I was just formulating my final conclusion that bank machines have caused us to be a nation of paranoiacs—afraid of
being pegged by the bank as a Major Loser undeserving of
cash, and then once we get the cash, terrified that we're going
to be robbed of it—when suddenly the man at the machine
turned to the crowd and pleaded for mercy.

He, it turned out, had been pegged a Major Loser and
needed to share his experience.

"I told the machine I wanted $60 and it spit out a receipt
showing it had *given* me $60, but no money came out," he
wailed.

Another man cleared his throat and said, "Maybe you
don't have the money in your account."

"That's right," added a no-nonsense woman in a business
suit. "The bank can tell, you know."

"But I *have* the money," the man said. He looked around,
hoping someone would believe him.

Let me just say that I believed him immediately. I know
how vicious those machines can be. Once, when I had innocently gone to collect cash, the bank machine, instead of
handing me the $20 I was desperate for, spit out a piece of
paper that said: "CARD CAPTURED."

Now what kind of mind game is this? Is this the Wild West
or something? I had to go into the bank—luckily it was open—
and stand in a line and plead for my card's release.

The bank manager gave me the level stare reserved for

Major Losers. "Why," she asked finally, "did you do something that made the machine capture your card?"

That's the kind of thing I'm talking about. And that's the way we all looked at the man who couldn't get his $60.

The man finally had to step aside, and Mrs. No-Nonsense marched up to the machine and pushed the buttons with certainty. The machine happily gave her cash—in fact, lots more than she'd asked for.

It was clear what had happened. The machine, in its wisdom, had decided she deserved all the man's money. She stood there for a moment, debating what to do, whether it was by divine law that she should have his money *and* her money, or if it was a simple machine malfunction.

After a few tough moments, she called to him and gave him a fistful of cash.

The crowd actually cheered and hugged the man. And everybody stood around for 10 extra minutes telling horror stories about bank machines.

If that's not bringing people together, I don't know what is.

The VCR Manual

I wish I was the kind of person who could sit down and read the manual to the VCR.

I know this is a stupid thing to wish for. It's not like the other things on my current wish list: world peace, an end to homelessness, and better hair.

Conceivably, I could just go into the living room, sit down on the couch, clear my throat, do some lumbar stretches, yawn, stand up, turn around in a circle three times, sit down and open the manual to page one, and just—read it.

But I can't.

Something happens to me when I come upon sentences like this one: "After pre-tuning, if you wish to change the real channel number to correspond to the actual pre-tuned station, press the CH NO. SET button after calling up the corresponding channel position number on the display and enter the desired channel number using the READ OUT buttons (10 and 1)."

I feel like slipping into a coma.

Luckily, though, I do the next best thing. I call Ben.

You see, back in 1976, when many of my friends were wasting time going to parties and waxing their cars, I—always with an eye to the future—was busy producing a 1990's teen-ager.

I like to think I had some sixth sense that the day would come when teen-agers were required to operate the world's technology and save us from having to read those horrible thick manuals that make no sense.

Don't ask me why it is that teen-agers understand this stuff *without* reading these manuals. No one knows why that is.

All I know is that if I get a yearning to record a TV show that's coming on three weeks from now on a Thursday, say at 4:30 a.m., I mention this fact to Ben, and he spends about 15 minutes punching buttons, spinning knobs, and bargaining with the gods of technology—and miraculously the show appears on my tape.

I am the envy of all my friends without teen-agers—people who think VCR clocks are *supposed* to be constantly flashing, and that "high speed dubbing" is how King Arthur knighted people when he was in a big hurry.

Lately when the phone rings, it's the neighbors wanting to know if Ben can dash over to retrieve their answering machine messages and tend to their compact disc programming needs.

A woman I barely know, but who had heard of Ben's consultations, actually needed him to reset all her household digital clocks after the daylight savings time change.

I was in complete sympathy. Still, I thought she should have been a little more apologetic about wasting all those years attending Grateful Dead and Fleetwood Mac concerts, when she could have been producing children who would have been able to explain a digital programming system to her someday.

Recently, my husband and I sat down to watch television, but the picture fizzed and blipped and spun across the screen. I knew immediately what needed to be done.

I woke Ben up out of a sound sleep and begged him to fix it.

He came shuffling downstairs, squinting in the light, and studied the set for a minute. Then he said, "Oh," and pressed a button *right on the front of the set*, and the picture was miraculously restored.

I didn't ask why that worked, or what that button did, or why TV sets would even have a button that could be pressed to mess up the picture and then pressed again to make it work.

I know to be silent when there's a communion with technology, and I'm a witness.

But the real truth is that I don't *want* to know.

There are times when Ben, more than anything, wants to *explain* it all to me. He starts sounding like the manual. "Just hold the B button down while you press the A button five times, and open this little door here where the tracking controls are, and turn this twice . . . "

I faint dead away onto the kitchen floor.

But that's not the tough part. I have to think of some way to break the news to Ben that he won't ever be allowed to leave home. It's an in-state college for him, and no late-night parties—unless he leaves a number where we can reach him at all times.

You never know when the VCR will need a tracking adjustment.

A Declaration of Life's Perfection

I haven't lived on this planet for so many years without learning a thing or two about life.

The main thing I've learned is that when all else is OK in your life, your car will jump in to fill the Trouble Vacuum. Cars can't stand it if you are bored a whole day, or when nothing hair-raising is happening to you.

In other words, don't let your car find out when a personal crisis finally passes. If you can't bring yourself to weep on the way to work each day, at least complain loudly enough for your car engine to hear.

Don't do what I did.

I was driving down Interstate 91, my two daughters in the car with me, when I suddenly realized that there were *no major problems* to be solved in the next hour and a half.

"This is absolutely amazing!" I said aloud, because I believe children need to hear about good fortune as often as possible. "There is nothing we're supposed to be worrying about! There isn't even a nursery school spring fair we have to think about!"

Three minutes later, we were standing on the side of the highway, next to our dead car.

The clutch had decided there was no point to its continued existence, since our lives were already so peachy. I can understand this attitude from an inanimate object, but what I can't forgive is that the car couldn't even wait one more lousy mile to dump us at the next exit.

No matter how wonderfully your life is going, you should-n't have to walk a mile on I-91 with a 4-year-old who hasn't had lunch yet.

Luckily, we didn't have to. We were trudging along the grassy area, when somebody's tenderhearted grandmother pulled over, complete with an air-conditioned car and a box of cookies.

"I haven't ever in my life picked up strangers on the road," she said, "but you three are the most pathetic-looking people I've ever seen. Get in."

She drove us to a hotel just off the next exit, where our pitifulness impressed the desk clerk into finding us a Coke machine and a pay phone.

My sister and her husband came, fetched us, and took us back to the car, where my sister's husband pronounced it dead, and where we all read the little orange sticker the state troopers had plastered on it, giving us 24 hours to remove the car.

Early the next morning, we called our saintly mechanic, who said he'd send a towing service for it and change his schedule around so he could fix it that day.

It was then that I made a probably fatal mistake. I slipped back into thinking that life was actually still wonderful. After all, the car would soon be fixed, we hadn't died on the high-way, and we still had no more nursery school spring fairs to think about. Then the mechanic called with just one question:

"Now *where* did you say your car is?"

It took a while to determine that the car had not decided simply to vanish—that it had, in fact, been towed by overzealous state troopers who decided that just this once they'd let that old cumbersome 24-hour rule slide.

We called towing services, we reasoned with the state troopers (who said they were very sorry), we called the me-chanic and arranged for towing again—and some 48 hours later, our car was fixed.

The bill was approximately one million dollars.

Apparently many of the car's systems had overheard my Declaration of Life's Perfection and had decided to follow the clutch's lead.

Just for fun, I was reading over all the items on the bill. (Fun has taken on a different meaning these days.) The car's disloyalties are all itemized there.

But down the bill a ways is an entry I really like. Underneath a smudge, it says: "Kleen—,$3."

Now I *know* this doesn't say Kleenex. Of *course* it doesn't say Kleenex.

But isn't that a great image anyway—all the mechanics standing around, so moved by our situation that they had to send out for $3 worth of Kleenex?

I laughed, hard. Too hard.

This morning I got in the car, forgot to complain about life, and discovered the car was dumping transmission fluid all over my foot.

Appliance Nuisances

I have always secretly suspected that machines are out to get me, and now I have proof.

The car has decided it no longer wants the role of Helpful Family Car. I was driving down the road, and it just stopped.

That's it. Halted in the middle of the road, stopped its engine, and waited. Said to me, in essence, "I am not going to go any farther. You can walk for all I care."

Well, luckily I know how to talk to a car that's in that mood. I've driven enough cranky used cars in my life to know what a car is asking for when it just stops in the middle of the road.

It wants wires. Distributor caps. And the kind of talk only a trained mechanic can give it.

But once I had provided all these things for that car, the *other* car got in a snit over no money having been spent on *it*. (Few people know that machines have a highly developed sense of sibling rivalry.)

The second car wanted new tires all around, or it threatened to have a major blowout.

Fine.

But somehow—even though I tried to be very discreet and not talk about car troubles within earshot of the house—the household machines caught wind of all these demands being met, and wanted in on the action.

Actually, I was resigned to this. You can't live in America without expecting a certain amount of Appliance Nuisance in life, and I don't get upset about it anymore. In fact, if I had to describe my mood of this week, I would say I was light-hearted, even though I was having to spend my days passing out new wires, occasional switches, and various other implements for all the mechanical devices in the house.

I would console myself and escape from this appliance hell by going off every chance I got and working on my novel.

One summer years ago, I started writing a novel, and ever since then, I go in and hack away at it whenever I have more than 15 consecutive minutes. This is a novel where people have lots more to think about than whether their car needs a new distributor cap—and so it's a great relief for me to go there.

When I'm lost in that novel, believe me, I get to say when the appliances break and when they don't.

So there I was, writing along at top speed and having a wonderful time engineering everyone's life into a flat-out catastrophe, when the computer crashed.

("Crash" is the technical term for the computer saying, "Write with a pencil for all I care.") The way my son, Ben, explained it when I stopped shrieking long enough to listen, my word processor thought that 316 pages was time enough for me to wrap up the catastrophes and get the plot settled, and that it simply wasn't going to write another word—and in fact, wasn't even going to let me *see* again any of the words I *had* written.

"You'll just have to use your back-up disk," he said cheerfully.

Is this the craziest thing you ever heard? As if I am the type of person who would have a back-up disk! I explained that I don't have the kind of mind that runs to making back-up disks.

"What is a back-up disk, anyway?" I said.

He sighed and then he did all kinds of special voodoo dances and incantations over the computer. He put in disks and tapped in magic spells, and I sat there, sure it was all going to work out fine and promising every few minutes that

I would *learn*, by God, what a back-up disk is, and I would make them *every day of my life*, if necessary, only please, processor gods, give me back my 316 pages.

"*Ha!*" said the computer. And then it came out with the deal it was willing to make—a deal so evil only a machine could have come up with it:

It gave me back my novel, only it had scrambled it all around, taking two sentences from here and mixing them up with three sentences from the middle, and then a couple of paragraphs from the end, and putting it all together—316 pages of this, like a giant jigsaw puzzle of words.

I haven't told the computer that I have a printout of most of the novel.

Still, I think I'll write the rest of it with my trusty pencil— as long as I don't have to go near the pencil sharpener.

Crazy about the Net

I don't mean to be one of those people who whines about progress, but surely we've all noticed that computers are taking over the world, and no one is even putting up a fuss about it.

Just look around. These days you can't even stand in line at the bank without someone telling you about CD-ROMS (not, I found out, a new kind of certificate of deposit), or discussing their Notebooks (which I also just found out are really laptop computers, not loose-leaf paper holders after all).

One very unsettling effect of this computer takeover is that it's caused people to start talking in initials and numbers.

When my friend Greg asked me if I had a PC at home, I actually had to think a minute what he could possibly be referring to. A politically correct?

A politically correct *what*?

"Oh," I said finally. "You mean a personal computer. Oh, yes, I do."

But he couldn't be satisfied with just knowing that. Noooooo. He then wanted to know if it was a 40 MHZ 486DX with desktop publishing, CAD-/CMA, UNIX/Xenix, and did it have Windows?

"You must have Windows," he said.

"It's next to the window," I said.

"Well, what MS-DOS do you have?"

I had to run and look at my computer. It was an 8088, with a 3.1 MS-DOS.

"You have an 8088?" he said. "Not a 386? Not even a 286? I would have pegged you for at least a 286!"

Computer people might as well know that this is just the kind of talk that makes them unpopular with the rest of us and keeps them from being invited to parties.

I had to let Greg know right then that I wasn't born yesterday, technologically speaking. I mean, I may be clip-clopping along with an 8088 sitting by the window, but I am actually the sort of person who knows a thing or two about the Information Superhighway.

"*You*?" he said. "You go on the Net?"

"I'm *crazy* about the Net," I said. "I'm on it all the time."

The truth is that I know how to do one thing on the Internet: check my e-mail. But it is just possible that I may be a legally certified e-mail addict at this point. That's how good I am at it.

My e-mailing partner is my friend Alice, who lives in San Francisco. We used to have a telephone relationship, but if you have ever tried to have a relationship with a California person, you probably know the difficulties. They *insist* on living their lives three hours earlier there.

You can never ever call them in the morning; they claim it's the middle of the night. Then, if you try to call them during your own nighttime, they are still at work and too busy to talk to you.

That's why e-mailing them is a good idea.

Well, my friend Alice is no more computer-literate than I am, but luckily we were both clever enough to give birth to sons some time ago—and so we both have been granted honorary entrance into cyberspace.

Picture this heart-warming scene from the '90s: *two* sons, on opposite coasts, working diligently to explain concepts like wordwrap to their impatient, uncaring mothers, who are snapping, "I don't want to know how the Internet works! I just want to write a note to my friend! Hurry up, will ya?"

My son ended up finally writing me out a list of instructions—a step-by-step guide that makes no sense to me whatsoever. I just push the buttons he says to push, and weird things flash up on the screen, and I pay no attention to them.

When I first sent her an e-mail message—well, it was like Alexander Graham Bell and Watson all over again. I actually had to call her up so we could congratulate each other long distance.

Since then, we've spent more in long-distance calls than ever, what with having to make sure that e-mail really does arrive where it's supposed to.

Recently we actually had two full exchanges—a message and a reply—without having to talk on the telephone.

So naturally I called her up so we could congratulate ourselves.

"We're really on it," I said. "We're on the Information Superhighway!"

"Yes," she said, "but we're walking on the highway. Everyone else is driving."

A Precarious Time for Cars

I don't want to sound like one of those people who blames her mother for everything, but the fact is I've had five major car disasters in one week. *And* my mother was visiting from Florida.

You can't just ignore a coincidence like that.

I don't know how my automotive life became all tangled up with my mother's visit, but trust me, it happened.

I should have suspected something when, as her plane touched down on the runway, the sky immediately turned black, an Oz-type wind whipped up, and by the time I was lugging her two massive lead-filled suitcases to the car, I had to dodge lightning bolts and leap over lakes.

We left the airport in a blinding rain—so blinding, in fact that the first highway sign I could actually read said: "Welcome to Massachusetts."

Mothers can be touchy about these kinds of mistakes, you know. An incident like this can often remind them of the time you dropped a plate into a neighbor's washing machine during the spin cycle, or when you were learning to drive and ran out of gas four times in one week.

But my mother stayed cheerful, even when it took 30 minutes to find a place to turn around. She said she'd always wanted to see Massachusetts.

So I thought we had dealt with our mother/daughter/car issues, but later that night, a nice man rang our door-bell to announce Disaster No. 2. He'd come along, he said, in time to see some kids running away from our car. When you live in a city, that's never a good sign.

Sure enough, the lock on the driver's side had been permanently jammed. The choices, as my mechanic has explained it, are: pay $85, or climb into the driver's seat through the passenger-side door.

In spite of the fact I opted for the difficulties of climbing through the passenger door, more Fun with Cars was lurking. This is against my personal theory of Life Problems, you see, which requires that one problem be completely solved before the next one comes along.

But the next one came anyway, in the form of tow trucks and parking tickets. We'd gotten so caught up in the lock-jamming problem that we neglected to move the cars in time for the street-sweeping—which was being held at the crack of dawn in honor of my mother's visit, no doubt.

"This is a very precarious time," I whispered to my husband. "Odd forces are at work here. We must be very careful of our *car keys.*"

He gave me a strange look—and an even stranger one six hours later when he arrived at the shopping center to rescue us.

My keys had simply vanished.

They weren't in the video store, where we had spent 45 minutes browsing, nor were they anywhere in the department store where we had tried on skirts, purses, shoes, hats, jewelry, and jackets for the rest of the afternoon.

My husband said what husbands always say at times like this: "Did you look in your purse?"

I didn't say that to him 24 hours later when his keys were lost.

We searched for over an hour—and then, because it was my mother and not his who was visiting, the fates decided to give his keys back.

I found them tucked underneath the back seat of the car, hiding behind a kid's book and a granola bar. There was, of course, no possible way they could have gotten there. No one holding those keys had been *near* the back seat in days.

Still, it was inspiring to think a lost object could actually return from the other side, so I called the video store and the department store yet again. I had barely said "hello," when the woman sighed and said, "Look. We. Don't. Have. Your. Keys."

We were making arrangements to replace the keys—and get some extra sets—when another tornado-laden thunderstorm blew in suddenly, forcing the entire family to take cover.

It wasn't until after it had gone that we remembered the car windows.

The seats were swamps.

But my mother was great about sitting on layers of towels to go back to the airport.

Given how things were going, I think she was just relieved we didn't have an accident on the way to the plane.

And when I got home, safe and sound, the department store called. They found my keys.

Social
Misunderstandings

Time for a New Hat

It's spring. I know this, not only because the television is full of March Madness, but also because when I put on my winter hat, it suddenly looks ridiculous.

Ridiculous in that way winter boots are ridiculous when you happen to bump into them in the back of your closet, say, in mid-July. You can't believe you went months putting these hideous objects on your own dear feet.

Obviously, it was time for a new hat.

And since it was my friend Alice's birthday—my local friend Alice, not my San Francisco Alice—I decided I would get *both* of us hats.

Naturally I forgot that I have a decision-making disorder, and figuring out which two hats to buy would probably kill me.

Just on the ride over to the store, I changed my mind and decided to buy Alice a T-shirt instead. But then the question became: short-sleeved or long? By the time I'd parked the car, I had decided on long, because short wouldn't be wearable for months. Only then I couldn't make up my mind whether it should be a long-sleeved T-shirt or a lightweight sweatshirt instead.

I could already see which way this day was going to go. Next I'd be mired in deeper questions: sweatshirt *with* writing or *without* writing? And this was all before we even got into what color, for God's sake.

"Hats," I told myself firmly. "You will buy hats."

Let me tell you right now, in case you are planning to do anything like this: there is absolutely nothing in the world more exhilarating than making a decision to buy two hats.

Luckily for me, the store I went into had only four kinds of hats to decide about, or I would be there still, sending out for meals.

The first one I saw was *the* perfect hat. It had tiny little flowers all over it and a great brim that you could flip up or down (Alice and I both like brims), and it didn't seem as if it would blow off in the wind or be ugly when wet.

I stood in front of the mirror for really an embarrassingly long time, trying on all the sizes. I flipped the brims all around every possible way, and when the saleswoman wasn't looking, I made some faces at myself and did my hair all around different ways.

I knew I would buy this hat. But for which one of us?

So then I did the same thing with the three other kinds of hats. Once, I looked over and saw the saleswoman watching me in astonishment. I had every hat in the store piled around me.

"Tough decision," she said.

I finally managed to rule out the off-white hat because it looked as if you'd have to play tennis to wear it. And the cream-colored one with blue somethings on it, which should have been terrific, just wasn't somehow.

But the beige was quite elegant and had the advantage over the flowered hat in that it would go with everything.

Flowers, I explained to myself, were almost too cute. Alice probably wouldn't want to be wearing little spring flowers.

I put all the hats back on the shelf and went searching for T-shirts. Then I got them all back again and tried them on once more. I saw the saleswoman smiling into her hand. So I marched up to the counter, to show I was a decision-making kind of person after all, and paid for the beige and the flowered one. I'd figure out later who should get which.

My husband said he liked the flowered one best.

"I had just this minute decided to give it to Alice," I told him.

He laughed.

When I went to meet Alice, I was wearing the flowered one, and I had the beige one in a bag. She stared at me.

"That is the most wonderful hat I've ever seen!" she said. I handed her the bag and mumbled something about happy birthday.

Immediately I could tell that she hated the beige one, that she thought it was the most boring-looking beige hat in the entire world. "Thank you," she said, politely.

So what could I do but tell her the whole story, and we both tried on both hats again, and we said the beige one looked great on me, and the flowered one looked great on her.

And then—we didn't even discuss it—I started up the car motor, and we drove back to the store, and went in and put the beige one back and got another flowered hat.

"People will laugh at us having the same hat," I said.

"So what?" she said. "They laugh at us already."

Dinner Parties

Judy, my friend from California, called the other day to tell me she has to move to a new state.

She sounded so sad I was afraid she'd lost her job. But no, it wasn't that. And yes, her house was still wonderful. The problem was *waaay* more insidious.

It was dinner parties.

"Ah," I said. "You have to move because it's your turn to give a dinner party."

She burst into tears. It seems that she's gotten herself mixed up with a bad crowd out there in sunny L.A.: the kind of people who can invite 60 of their dearest friends over for supper and actually *give* them food, without so much as breaking out in a sweat.

Judy and I aren't the kind of people who can do this. When guests come to my house expecting to be fed, chances are that, at some point, they're going to find themselves wearing oven mitts. At the very least, they'll be setting the table and answering a few telephone calls.

Judy may be even worse. Once, when she invited me over for dinner, I showed up at the appointed hour of 7:30 p.m. only to find out that we'd be starting with a trip to the supermarket, where we had to buy a *frozen* package of hamburger and a cookbook. I think we got around to eating at about 10:45 that night.

I could see how she might be panicking.

"If I don't move right now," said Judy, "I figure I'll have to give about 10 dinner parties before summer."

The people she knows in L.A. don't know how close to starvation they may be edging.

Oh, but dinner parties are nothing to be sneered at. The worst one I ever had was years ago when I got stuck having all the day-care families over to my house for a potluck supper.

Now that just shows my bad attitude. I shouldn't say "got stuck." I think I may have even volunteered. I'm sure I was thinking it wouldn't be so bad, being potluck and all. Everybody would bring something.

The trouble was that nobody ever got around to writing anything down on the Potluck Food Sign-Up Sheet. You remember the '80s, don't you—fear of commitment and all that? As soon as everybody started to arrive, it became clear that the worst had happened.

Fifteen families showed up, 14 of them bringing paper plates and cups. Only one family brought anything resembling food, and *that* was a sliced cucumber sprinkled with dill flakes.

The truly embarrassing part of the evening came when we all foraged for food in my cabinets and turned up only a box of Raisin Bran and a can of peas.

We ended up piling into cars and going out for pizza. That's when I discovered that the only kind of dinner party to have is one that can move to a pizza restaurant.

Equally hideous was the time some friends invited us for dinner and assigned us to bring salad and dessert. In fact, for the entire week before the Big Event, they called us every day to talk *more* about the arrangements.

The government should be run as carefully as this meal was being planned. We got to the point where we could barely stand to take their calls. Should it be green salad or potato salad? Hot and gooey dessert or cold and creamy? Chicken, certainly, and some kind of potato. Juice for the kids.

I actually ended up putting the rest of my life on hold

while I mapped out my salad and dessert plans. Being specific seemed to be the key to keeping the phone from ringing.

When we got to their house, proudly carrying a tossed salad and apple crisp, we were met with a stunned silence. *Where*, they wanted to know, was the roasted chicken we'd promised to bring? And the potatoes?

It turned out they had made the salad and dessert. I remember walking home later that night, puzzling over the whole thing. *We* were the guests, and yet *we* were the ones supposed to bring the chicken and potatoes? It didn't seem right.

"Why didn't they just invite themselves over to *our* house for dinner?" my husband wanted to know. "At least then we wouldn't have had to carry our pots and pans through the streets."

Who knows? That's just the way dinner parties go. Always bizarre.

I'm beginning to think Judy may be right. It'd be far easier to move than to contemplate another dinner party like that. And believe me, her friends in L.A. will thank her.

A Standing Ovation

My friend Diane edits a national magazine, manages a team of writers, and understands why people need fax machines in their cars. But I had her flat-out amazed by eight bags of groceries.

She came to visit just as I was getting back from Stop & Shop.

"What are you going to do with these?" she asked. I always have to remind myself that Diane is a single person who thinks food only comes in little take-out boxes.

"Well," I said, "these are groceries. First I'm going to put them away on the shelves, and then later I'll take some of them down and cook them on the stove. We'll eat the cooked food to get nourishment."

"This is unbelievable!" she said. "This much food must have cost you $100!"

"Actually," I said modestly, "it was more like $135.63. But it's for the whole week."

She swooned. "I don't see how you do it. First you go to the store and come back with all this stuff, and now during the week you have to *cook* all of it? How in the world will you manage to do all this?"

The fact is I spend quite a few hours each day asking myself that very question about one thing or another, so it's always a relief when someone else speaks it out loud and I don't have to ponder it in silence.

This is one of the main reasons I love it when Diane comes

to visit. She makes my daily life sound so *interesting*, as though I must be a five-star genius to raise three kids and make sure they all get something to eat every day and learn not to play on the highway during rush hour.

She's always saying something like, "I think it's just incredible the way you gave Stephanie a hug when she fell down, to make her stop crying!" or: "How do you ever keep track of everyone's laundry?"

She even finds the contents of my car fascinating. I'll catch her digging through the remains of granola bars, one-legged baby dolls, and Sesame Street books, acting like an archaeologist at a dig site.

"How did you ever learn to anticipate what all these children are going to need in the car?" she'll say.

I particularly love it when she calls them "all these children," because there are lots of days when each of them is 10 children apiece, and as anyone can tell you, 30 children is a lot of people to mother.

Everybody needs someone like Diane to come to their house.

My friend Jennifer, a writer who also has three children, has a couple of childless women friends who sometimes stay overnight at her house. They sit at the table in the morning and marvel at the way Jennifer fixes breakfast, hands out lunch money, produces lost shirts and socks, and remembers the locations of homework assignments.

As the children leave, one by one, these friends have even taken to calling out, "Launch One! Launch Two! Launch Three!"

And then they give Jennifer a standing ovation.

In these days when parents generally get a bad rap and have inferiority complexes all over the place, I think a standing ovation is long overdue. Until Diane came along to applaud me for being clever enough to carry a lot of junk in my car, I had to content myself with thoughts of revenge toward previously childless people who are now experiencing the true test of parenthood.

Like my cousin Linda, for instance. As a bored teen-ager,

she would hang around my house, critically observing my attempts to wrangle two toddlers into becoming respectable citizens.

"It's so good that I'm able to watch you and learn from all the mistakes you're making," she said to me once. Later, she protested that she meant this in the nicest way possible.

But the fates took swift revenge. Linda now has two children under 2 years old, whom she described in her hastily scribbled Christmas note as "incredible monsters."

I should stop chuckling about it, I know. If I were really a kind person, I'd recommend my friend Diane go over to visit.

Linda would probably appreciate someone thinking she's terrific for even managing to write a note.

Pick a Date

"So when shall we get together?" said Alice. The fact was, we were *already* together, having tea downtown on a Monday afternoon. She meant when could we get together in the *formal* sense—husbands and all, for dinner in a restaurant. Sort of a holiday thing.

Let's just say this is a personal challenge— lining up such an event.

Even getting ourselves to stick to the subject is a personal challenge.

"I don't know," I said. "Let me get my calendar."

I started rummaging through my purse, which meant taking out most things I own because my calendar is down at the very bottom.

Alice was plainly impressed by how much stuff fits into my purse.

"Isn't that the wallet you bought when I bought that red one?" she asked. "Wasn't that back in 1985?"

It was. It is one of my life's accomplishments that I have managed to keep my wallet alive for so long, even though it's the Velcro kind, and everyone knows that Velcro gets tired from little pieces of tissue sticking to it all the time.

Some days, in fact, this is the only accomplishment I can point to with any certainty.

Alice and I did a full five minutes on Velcro Horror Stories—such as the things that happen to children's Velcro sneakers—and then three minutes on my Velcro Wallet Success Story.

Then she said, "So when shall we get together?"

"The calendar!" I said, and went through my purse again. I have one of those black spiral Weekly Minders, worn out now from a year of being used.

"How many lines does your calendar give you per day?" Alice wanted to know.

We looked. It has nine, but they're skinny lines. It's the kind of calendar that assumes that your life stops after 5 p.m.

After two minutes devoted to the short-sighted assumptions of calendar manufacturers, we moved on to Alice's calendar problems, which are basically that she didn't have her calendar until a few days ago, because she was waiting to see if her friend Lorraine was going to give her one like she did last year.

"It was such a great calendar— lots of lines for everything you can think of— that I didn't want to go out and buy an inferior one if she was going to give me one, and I couldn't very well call her up and ask her. So I've been unable to plan anything for weeks," she said.

This led us off on a discussion of gifts: what are good ones, how soon before the holidays should they be delivered, and does one incur an obligation to give the same useful gift year after year when people might be counting on it.

After a lengthy discussion, we decided people do have this obligation.

Then I said, "So when are we getting together?"

That unfortunately brought us right back to calendars because, while Alice did eventually get her calendar from her friend, she doesn't exactly want to carry two calendars with her, which is what you have to do in late November.

Having two calendars, as anyone will tell you, can potentially lead to all kinds of neck pain. This reminded me that I learned a new neck exercise in my yoga class, which led us to discussing yoga, yoga teachers, and clothing to be worn while doing yoga. Finally I just stood up and demonstrated the exercise right there at the table.

"Why is this so hard?" she asked.

"It's really a very simple exercise," I said.

"No," she said. "Why is it so hard to stay on this conversation about when we're going to get together?"

We decided it's because we've known each other so long, and so at any given time, we've always got the threads of about 30 conversations hanging in midair, ready to be taken up again at a moment's notice.

As far as we know, in the 16 years of our friendship, we have never once completed a conversation we've started. We're actually *bogged down* in unfinished topics.

"Men finish conversations," she pointed out. "Why can't we?"

This led back to one of our all-time favorite conversations— why men and women are so different and what can or should be done about it.

It was, as usual, inconclusive.

I finished my last bit of tea, and we walked out to our cars and said goodbye.

"I'll have my husband call your husband," she said, "and we'll get this nailed down."

Civilization's Decline

You will not believe what happened to my friend Cindy, even though I swear this is really true.

She was invited to dinner at her friend Kim's house, which would have been wonderful, except that the day before the dinner, Cindy's 10-year-old had a fever and Cindy didn't think she should leave him with a sitter.

So she called Kim up and said, "Why don't you come here instead?"

Kim said that would be fine and insisted on bringing the main course, since she'd already made a chicken curry dish that she's famous for.

"Great," said Cindy. "Bring it along, and I'll make rice and a salad."

"Oh, and my friend Joe will bring the bread," said Kim.

Well, this was all fine, and things simply could not have been nicer—except that when Kim showed up for dinner, all 16 of her *other* dinner guests came along, too.

Sixteen unexpected dinner guests.

Cindy nearly had to be pharmaceutically revived.

So what Cindy wanted to know from me was, at what point was she supposed to have been able to figure out that this was not an intimate dinner with Kim, Cindy and a guy named Joe?

"What did I miss?" she said to me. "Where was the signal?"

Well, I don't know why the heck she's asking me. As a person who owns *possibly* 16 plates altogether, with most of them underneath potted plants throughout the house, I have to admit this story gave me the chills. I could picture myself running around collecting dirt-caked plates and explaining how they'd wash up real nice, while 16 of somebody else's dinner guests watched.

I mean, if this kind of thing can happen, then obviously we don't have a civilization anymore.

That's what I told my friend Lizzie when I recounted the story to her, and she said I should calm down about it, because these kinds of social misunderstandings are rampant.

Why, just a few weeks before, she and her kids had gone off to dinner at some friends' house, and when they got there, the friends were not home, there was obviously no dinner cooking, and they knew with a dreadful certainty that they had come on the wrong day.

They were perfectly willing to creep away quietly, except for one thing: Lizzie's husband was supposed to meet them there.

The problem now became: If they waited for him, no doubt the hosts would come home, and they'd feel so bad about the misunderstanding that they'd insist on making dinner and go to lots of trouble and then Lizzie would feel *awful*, etc., etc.

Well, they couldn't decide what to do. They couldn't stay put and they couldn't park elsewhere on the street to wait for the husband because no doubt the hosts would come along, spot their car, and then they'd really have a lot of explaining to do.

So Lizzie and her kids did the only possible thing: They drove a while to a place where they were sure her husband would pass, and waited for him there, to flag him down and explain the situation.

Only it was so dark they couldn't really spot his car. The oldest son had to flag down each passing car— in the freezing cold— to make sure it wasn't his father's.

After about 10 cars, there was finally a lull. The son got back in the car, looked over at Lizzie and said, "Well, at least we've got our health."

And that, says Lizzie, sums up social misunderstandings. They make you think you've lost your mind.

I'm afraid my worst social misunderstandings are tame by comparison.

Once, we were invited to a dinner, and when we got there with our salad and apple crisp, it turned out that was also what the hosts had made.

God knows how this had happened. But slowly— very slowly and painfully— it dawned on everyone that there was not going to *be* any roasted chicken, green beans or mashed potatoes. Just *lots* of salad and apple crisp.

My family kept flashing me weird looks, like this was another one of *my* oddball ideas of a decent meal. So when the hosts left the room for a moment, I tried to whisper to them about social misunderstandings and the downfall of civilization and all the rest of it.

And then— well, we left when we could and went to a restaurant.

Sometimes that's the best way.

A Personal Triumph

It was a personal triumph of sorts for me. I reached both Susan *and* Madeline on the telephone.

Ordinarily I set my standards for Personal Triumphs a bit higher than just getting phone conversations going, but these had been teetering for so long on the brink of about-to-happen-but-somehow-not-happening that they had achieved almost mythic proportions in my life.

My children and office mates had given up saying hello to me anymore; instead they said, "Oh, Susan called," or sometimes, for variety, "Madeline wants you to call her back."

It had gotten to be like some kind of joke.

Who *were* Susan and Madeline, what did they *want* from me, and exactly what was the telephonic impediment that kept us from ever actually speaking to each other on the phone?

Here's how it started:

I got to work one morning and there was one of those pink phone message slips on the desk. It said, "Call Susan."

I wasn't sure who Susan was, but I dialed the phone number on the slip and, naturally, got an answering machine. So I left a message for Susan to call *me*. And then I went to the cafeteria and got a cup of tea.

When I got back, there was another pink message slip saying, "Call Susan."

So I called her again, and this time got a busy signal.

During the 10 seconds I was listening to Susan's busy signal, Madeline called and left a message for me with the message desk.

Madeline is an old friend who calls once a year. So I called her back— and got *her* answering machine. I left a message and gave her my two phone numbers, home and work.

By then it was lunch time.

When I got back from lunch, both Susan and Madeline had called. Madeline had left a message that she'd try me at home. Susan had said she was going to be out and would call tomorrow.

When I got home from work, the children said Madeline had called and would call me later.

Call *later*?

Anyone who has in her house a combination of teen-agers and computer modems knows that calling later just isn't going to work out. My phone is occupied well into the night with uploading and downloading.

So, before the Modem Hours kicked in, I made a quick call to Madeline to see what she wanted. No answer.

Just to see, I dialed Susan's number. Busy.

And then I lost interest.

But the next day we all did it again. And the next, and the next and the next.

I left messages, they left messages. We all apologized several times for the difficulties.

I started putting these phone calls on my List of Things to Do: "Call Susan and find out what she wants. GET MADELINE ON THE PHONE ONCE AND FOR ALL!!"

I even dreamed that Susan called and I couldn't get to the phone, and a voice said, "That was Susan for the one-millionth time, and now you'll never know what she wanted!"

"I don't really care what she wanted," I explained in the dream. "I just want a day when I don't get a message to call her back."

Maybe that's when the tide turned, as they say. I quit apologizing to answering machines. Once, speaking to Susan's answering machine, I heard myself saying, "I'm not really all *that* hard to reach. I don't know why this isn't working out!"

And once Madeline, in a voice that was clearly bristling, said on my answering machine, "Why do people call other people and then immediately leave the building?"

She was a fine one to talk.

But then, for some reason, the world loosened its grip on us momentarily. The telephone rang, and when I picked it up, it was Susan on the phone.

"Hi," she said. "Do you remember me? We worked together at an insurance company back in the early 1980s."

"I didn't work at an insurance company in the early 1980s," I said.

"Oh, no!" she said. "You mean this whole ordeal was for nothing?"

But the thing with Madeline worked out fine. She's got a new job and a new boyfriend. We had lots to talk about.

She wants to have lunch together, just as soon as she gets back from vacation.

She said she'll call me.

A Gender Thing

Rib Removal

Raising daughters is different from raising sons. I know this may break the hearts of some of you, who no doubt are thinking that if you just get the Right Toys in the house, you can bring up everybody the same way.

I'm sorry. You can't.

If you have a daughter, trust me, from the time she is 3 weeks old, she is thinking, "Hmmm, this is the same sweater I spit up on last time. Doesn't this woman have any *variety* to her wardrobe?"

Go ahead. Give her all the G.I. Joe figures you can afford. There will still be the day when you find she painted G.I. Joe's toenails pink and dressed the cat in your finest underwear, complaining that it isn't nicer.

I'm sure I don't have to point out that a boy would never think of doing that.

As the mother of two daughters, ages six and 15, I am used to coming home and having one of them say something to me along the lines of: "You know, one of your socks seems slightly darker than the other and the hemline of your coat sags a little."

Recently, I got a shock on how badly things have deteriorated. The six-year-old, Stephanie, said to me in a nonchalant voice, "So. Have you ever had a rib removed?"

"Of course not," I said.

"Hmmm," she said. "I'm a little surprised to hear that."

Well, I was surprised to hear that *she* was surprised, because frankly I don't know anyone who has undergone rib removal for any reason whatsoever. But she assured me that it was something people do all the time.

"One of my friends told me that Janet Jackson had two ribs removed so she would be skinny. And I said to her, 'So *that's* why I don't look like Janet Jackson,' " Stephanie told me.

As a modern-day mother, I am always on the alert for Female Self-Deprecation, so I launched into my lecture series on how we must learn to accept ourselves the way we are, that we are all imperfect in some way, but that we love ourselves and each other anyway, and wouldn't it be boring if everyone was perfect all the time. I ended with the heartfelt assurance that rib removal was not the path to everlasting joy.

I couldn't quite believe I was having to use my best self-esteem material on such a threat as rib surgery, but that's the way it is these days.

Instead of being impressed, as I had expected, Stephanie just said, "Well, how did you stay skinny and keep all your ribs?"

You can see that things are in a very bad way indeed, and that when you are raising daughters, you have to be constantly explaining the oddest bits of information.

A few days later, my friend Elsa came to visit. She had just marked her 35th birthday, and to celebrate—if you can call it that—she had gone to the dermatologist to make sure she wasn't wrinkling too fast.

Stephanie and I were both dumbfounded that someone would go to the doctor on account of a birthday.

"Why do you care about wrinkles?" Stephanie wanted to know.

"I just don't want to look old before I have to," Elsa said. "I want to take care of myself."

"So you must have kept all your ribs, like my mom did," said Stephanie.

Elsa looked a little taken back, but she admitted that her ribs were still intact. So then we told her the Janet Jackson rumor and how important it was to love yourself, even down to your last rib.

"My mom takes care of herself," said Stephanie. "She kept all her ribs, and she puts cream on her face."

She came over and put her arms around me. "Do you know what age you look?" she said to me sweetly. "When I look at you, I think to myself, 'There's a woman who's got to be 57 years old. That's how well she takes care of herself.' "

All I could say was thanks.

I tried to say it nicely.

Scoring at the Supermarket

I have wasted valuable years of my life wondering what men talk about when they're alone together.

I always assumed they were mostly talking about sex, with sports scores running a close second, followed by The Rundown of Exciting Plays from Last Weekend's Game. Then maybe if they got around to it, they latched onto regional statistics for car thefts, how big their muscles could get if they worked out, and then probably back to sex again. I was wrong on all counts.

Women out there, be aware: men are talking about their coupons.

These men are not wimps, either. I would never want to cast aspersions on people who get excited about little pieces of paper with "35 cents off" written on them, especially since I have personally never managed to get even *one* usable, non-expired coupon to the grocery store.

No. When men talk about coupons, they do it in the most manly way possible.

I actually overheard this conversation taking place in my own home between my husband and a friend of his. I admit that I was eavesdropping, hoping for some insight into the inner sanctum of men's brains.

I tiptoed to the door, thinking I might hear the secret of how car engines work. I thought it was possible I might even learn what "dump the DH" means.

Instead, I heard my own husband saying, "So, uh, this

week I managed to shave eight bucks off the grocery bill with coupons."

"Not bad," said his friend.

"Whaddya mean, not bad? You do any better?"

"Well, I average 13, 14 bucks a week. Course I'm down from the 22, 23 I was doing a coupla months ago."

"You must be getting doubles to do that well," said my husband. There was no mistaking the envy in his voice.

There was a dramatic pause. His friend cleared his throat and said, "*Triples*, my friend."

I was fascinated. It was actually the first time I'd been able to think about coupons for longer than 30 seconds without drifting into a coma.

Then they started bragging about the great new products couponing had led them to drag home.

"We're drinking passion fruit kiwi lime juice for every meal now," said my husband's friend. "With the two-for-one-deal, plus the 50 cents off coupon tripled, I figure they're *paying* my family to drink the stuff." Now is this a gender thing, or what? I have never in my life had a conversation with a woman about coupons without both of us ending up feeling guilty and inadequate.

Women see coupons for what they are: a slap in the face, a reminder that we are imperfect beings forced to live in a world which values cutting out and carrying around little slips of paper for weeks on end, and remembering to use them.

"Do you . . . save coupons?" I asked my friend Jennifer a few days later.

I thought she was going to burst into tears. "I try, I really try," she said. "But if I ever *do* remember to actually cut out one of the damn things and put it in my purse, then I can never find it at the checkout counter when I actually get around to finding the product. And if I hold up the line while I search for it, then the coupon's either in shreds or the checker says, 'This expired yesterday.' "

"Exactly," I said. Soon we were comparing coupon failure stories: the times we watched, stunned, as people checked out 10 bags of groceries for $5.98; the hand-lotion-at-the-bottom-of-the-purse fiascos that creamed our hard-won shreds of coupons; the times we've sprung for the gourmet frozen food because we had a coupon, only to find it was for the wrong size.

We had plenty of sad stories. Jennifer then told me about her uncle, a coupon whiz, who has no less than 200 cans of tuna fish at his house, and some of them cost him only *4 cents each.*

We sat in awed silence, sipping the passion fruit kiwi lime juice that our household now owned five bottles of.

"Men don't have these problems," I said.

"They just don't talk about them," she said.

Just then my husband came into the room with his file folders bulging with coupons.

"You won't believe it!" he said, pulling on his jacket. "I found a two-for-one on macadamia nut spaghetti sauce, but it expires in 10 minutes. I'm gonna go for it! See ya later!"

I didn't have the heart to tell him the car needed gas.

Blocks vs.
Dramatic Play

If I ever get tired of writing newspaper stories for a living, I figure I can always get a job as a wedding consultant in a day-care center.

As far as I know, this is an untapped market, but I think it could really take off.

After all, *nobody* on the planet thinks more about weddings than 4-year-old girls. They can't so much as eat their dinner without draping their paper napkin on their heads and humming "Here Comes the Bride" four or five times.

Believe me, this can be hard to watch day in and day out, particularly if you're the kind of conscientious mom who's trying to raise a female math major. My 4-year-old daughter, Stephanie, has been trying to get her own wedding off the ground for quite a while, and I'm stunned at how difficult it's been.

Choosing a bridegroom was the hardest part. Obviously. You can't rush into a momentous decision like that, especially when the cast of eligible bachelors is more interested in playing Batman than in helping you line up caterers and florists.

But finally she came home and announced she was getting married to Pierre—a guy who distinguished himself from the usual pack at day-care by performing wild Michael Jackson impersonations each day after lunch.

"I *love* the way he dances," she said.

Come on now. That's not the worst reason to pick one man over another. I've heard *lots* worse.

"Have the two of you already decided to get married?" I asked.

"Well," she said, "I told him we were getting married, and he said OK. He told me to pick a day."

Ah. The old you-pick-the-day-and-I'll-show-up scenario. I could have told her where that would lead.

And sure enough, Stephanie has picked just about every day for a month, but Pierre—*weelllll*, Pierre just isn't ready yet.

One day, Stephanie climbed into the car to go home from day-care and said, with a sigh, "Well, we're *still* not married."

"Why not?" I said. "I thought Pierre wanted to get married to you."

"Every time I tell him it's our day to get married, he's so surprised he can't think about it," she said.

"So what are you going to do?"

"Today I tried to get him to have the wedding, and he said no, so I said I'd draw him a picture if he'd marry me, and he said we could get married tomorrow. He said he's going to write me a letter tonight," she said.

This does not sound good. I wanted to caution her about signing any restrictive pre-nuptial agreements—after all, the Michael Jackson Impersonator's business could eventually become as big as the Elvis Business—but then she leaned forward and told me the real problem.

"Pierre," she said, dropping her voice confidentially, "doesn't like to go in the Dramatic Play area, where the wedding dress and veil are. And I'm not allowed to take those clothes into the Blocks Area. Sometimes I stand in the Dramatic Play area and call him, but he won't come."

"Why do you think that is?" I said.

"I know why it is," she said. "He's scared about it."

I've seen this kind of Marriage Phobia in 4-year-old boys before. My friend Jennifer's son once burst into tears at breakfast and could not be consoled, though Jennifer and her husband tried for a very long time.

What they finally got out of him, between sobs, was that some 4-year-old day-care tot had her hooks in him, and he believed he had to marry her that very day, and it was going to last *forever*.

"And I don't know what I'll do if I meet somebody else!" he kept wailing.

Lots of people worry about that kind of thing, and most of them are a lot older than 4.

But Stephanie, like most little girls obsessed with weddings, isn't too concerned about that. In fact, she told me at bedtime that Pierre just may not work out, and she might have to marry Jimmy instead.

Jimmy's willing and he doesn't mind going into the Dramatic Play area. There's only one problem: when they play together at daycare, he insists on being her cat.

"All he says to me is 'Meow,' " she said. "I pet him on the back."

As the wedding consultant, I have just one piece of advice: Hold off on the caterer for a while.

Dating

It must have been all the melting snow that caused some of my brain's memory banks to thaw out as well.

Suddenly, from the deep recesses, there was a huge patch in my brain that remembered *dating!*

You know: a time when a man and a woman go out together in the evening without their children. They eat dinner, maybe they go dancing or to see a movie. They hold hands. They smile. They talk to each other.

I described the process to my husband, and he immediately remembered it too. "Let's try it," I said. "Maybe this is something we could do."

We got so exhilarated over the idea of actually leaving the house for a purpose other than going to work or buying more snow shovels that we were inspired to go outside and chip away at the glacier in our driveway.

Going out on a date was obviously idiotic. We have three children, after all.

Ben, the oldest, announced he had an Extremely Important Project for school he had to work on all day long in the computer lab.

Allie, the middle kid, reminded us that she was committed to going to a friend's birthday party that night.

It was too bad, they said, that neither one would be around to baby-sit with Stephanie, who is 5.

But I was still in my I-can-solve-anything-because-later-I'm-going-to-get-out-of-this-place mood. "No, no, no! This is actually perfect!" I announced. "I'll leave now and take Ben to the computer lab, where he can work all day on his project. Then I'll pick him up later to come home and baby-sit Stephanie.

"After that, we'll leave for our date, drop Allie off at her party, go out to dinner, see a movie, and then pick Allie up from her party."

"But what if I come with you now to drop Ben off," said Allie, "and then we can stop and buy a birthday present for the party, and then we can take me to get my hair cut?"

"And I'll come too," said Stephanie, "because I want to eat lunch at the kind of place where they have cheese Danishes and I want to stop at a pet store and buy food for the goldfish so he won't die."

"OK, and I'll drop our roll of film off to be developed, and get the car washed," I said.

You can probably see the way things were heading. For some reason, I couldn't. Maybe I was too delirious over the prospect of dating my husband.

We took off, only to find that everybody was starving. So we stopped at Wendy's (unfortunately, no cheese Danishes). Then we dropped Ben off at the computer lab. We drove to the bank to get another wheelbarrow-load of money and took Allie to get her hair cut and to drop the film off.

Then we went to the CD store to get a gift certificate for the party person and to the pet store for fish food.

When we got home, after the car wash, we discovered that the party was from 5 p.m. to 8 p.m., and not in the later evening as we had thought. There would be no dropping Allie off on the way to dinner and a movie.

"Our date isn't going to work out, is it?" said my husband. It was 4:45.

"Well," I said. "I'll drive Allie to her party now, and then I'll come back for you, and then you and Stephanie and I can go have dinner somewhere, and then we can pick up both Allie and Ben, drive all three kids home, and then we'll go out for our date."

"So Stephanie's going on our date?" he said.

"Just the dinner part. The movie part is still just us."

We found a nice restaurant downtown, but guess what! No cheese Danishes. A small riot ensued. We threatened the rioter with No More Dinners Out, but by then, it was 8 o'clock—no food yet—and my husband left to pick up Allie.

He didn't seem to mind that his food was cold when he got back. No time to eat it anyway, before the movie started. We raced to pick up Ben, drove 15 miles home to drop all the kids off, and, with seven minutes to go, hurried off to the theater.

I think I remember smiling and holding hands before the movie started. But then I fell asleep.

A Five-Pound Sack of Flour

Hard as this may be to believe, I've been asked to be a grandmother to a five-pound sack of flour.

Those of you with children will instantly know that the school system is behind this. Hardly ever in Real Life does anyone ask you to dress up a sack of flour in baby clothes and then make sure it's never out of your sight.

But this is all in the name of teaching middle school kids that babies are a lot of work, which is certainly a worthy goal. However, the main lesson we in our house have learned is that a sack of flour wears 6-month-old size pajamas.

Our secondary lesson has been that flour sacks need to wear hoods at all times, or else their little makeshift heads will roll right off.

It's been a great time so far.

Actually, I've learned something even more important from this little social experiment.

Men, it seems, are changing.

This flour-sack-as-baby deal involves boys, too, of course. In fact, the class gets divided up into couples, and each couple must figure out a way to take care of their flour child.

Believe me when I tell you that, right at this minute, there are boys in New Haven playing basketball while sacks of flour clad in frilly dresses wait at the sidelines.

And—perhaps this is the most amazing part—there are boys who go to junior high school each day and find themselves pushing strollers to math class, changing baby outfits at lunch hour, and lugging flour-filled carseats onto the schoolbus.

Is this the 1990s, or what?

Frankly, I'm stunned.

I wasn't surprised at all when Allie, our 14-year-old, came home from school with this assignment. I didn't even blink when she and her friend, Esme, took off to the store to select their babies from the baking section.

"Did you get a King Arthur or a Pillsbury baby?" I asked. As the grandmother, I thought it would be a good idea to show interest.

But brand name wasn't important, they told me sternly. "What you want to look for in a baby is that it has a nicely glued seam at the bottom," Allie said. "You don't want a baby that leaks."

Indeed.

I watched, amused, as they rummaged through the box of old baby clothes looking for the perfect ensemble.

Naturally there were some tough decisions—questions we real parents have been blessed with never having to face. Do flour babies need shoes? And is it too distracting that flour sacks come without heads, and if so, what in the world could be used to make a realistic head?

And then there were questions of style. One of Allie and Esme's friends, they told me, was heading to Baby Gap after school to get a color-coordinated outfit. Other girls were planning to buy toys, bottles, pacifiers, and special kid-carrying baskets.

"Are boys doing this too?" I asked.

"They have to," said Allie grimly.

Well, I needn't have asked. It turns out there's never *been* a more involved group of young fathers. They did everything but ask for parental leave from school so they could tend their offspring.

And in fact, it was the father of Allie's little Pillsbury child who managed to manufacture a suitable head for their baby. He worked long into the night, creating a head out of a balled-up sheet, and then carefully drew features.

And get this: He even washed the baby's clothes and blanket! Come on now. No one's ever heard of a teen-age boy who knows how to work a washing machine and dryer. When we got the baby back, for our turn at joint custody, the baby was sparkling clean.

My friend Suzanne was amazed when I told her. "Tell Allie to keep in touch with this guy," she advised.

Still, I'm not sure we can say this experiment really worked. I mean, wasn't the point to show kids what a nuisance baby-care could be? Instead, it turned into kind of an art project—Competitive Baby Decorating, perhaps.

Next time, they need to devise something that really puts junior parents to the test.

I have in mind a bag of flour that really *does* leak—over and over again, ruining pair after pair of Baby Gap jeans. And then maybe attach some noise-making device that screeches every few hours all night long.

Then we'll see how many guys want to take their babies to the basketball court.

The Clean Team

We got to the movie theater early and were lounging in the plush velvet seats, munching popcorn, when I dropped the bomb.

There was no easy way to deliver this news, you understand. But I felt firmly that it wasn't something a woman should keep from her husband.

I turned and looked him right in the eye.

"I've decided to become a member of the Clean Team," I said. "We're going to have a clean house at last."

You know how husbands are. Take them out to a movie, and they can hear any amount of bad news with a smile on their faces.

He smiled at me, uncomprehending. "The Clean Team? What's that?"

"It's just a . . . method," I said. "Nothing you need to be concerned about, really. It's a way of . . . doing things. That I'll be doing."

The lights went down in the theater, but he wanted to hear more.

"What does this all mean? The Clean Team? This doesn't mean you're going to start scrubbing everything, does it?" he whispered.

"Don't get all worked up," I whispered back. "It's a way of keeping the house clean; that's all. Nothing basically will change. I've been reading a book about it and now I've ordered some products."

"You've been reading a book about cleaning the house?"

I hadn't wanted him to know this part actually, but yes, I *had* been reading a book about cleaning the house. I knew this was a ridiculous thing to do, so, I confess, I had sneaked around, reading the book only when no one else was around.

To be perfectly honest about it, I had started the book thinking this was something I could make fun of. A whole book devoted just to getting the house clean! What would people do to make a buck?

But then—how to explain this? Somewhere around the time I got to the chapter on "Countertop Problems," it all started making sense to me. I was also a person with counter-top problems. This book was talking to *me*.

Still, I hid it from my family. I read the chapter "Managing Your Feather Duster" late at night while I was in the bathtub, with the door locked. I didn't want to have to explain.

In the movie theater, the music started thundering and the screen lit up for coming attractions, but I could sense him staring at me.

"And now you've ordered products?" he whispered, still smiling.

"I've ordered the basic set."

"Products that will clean the house?"

"Yes."

"Similar to the ones we have under the sink in the kitchen?"

Isn't this just like men? It's no wonder some women have to sneak around. I told him we'd talk about it after the movie, hoping he'd forget. But as soon as the last credit flitted across the screen, he was back, wanting to hear all about the Clean Team. So I told him.

"The first thing you get is a little apron," I said.

"You sent away for an apron?"

"Not an ordinary one. It comes with a 12-inch tempered steel scraper and a three-position retractable razor blade holder. And a special pocket with a plastic liner for the debris you pick up around the floor."

He was nodding, the way psychiatrists do. But I went on.

"And little loops on the side."

"Loops?"

"For hanging spray bottles on."

"Spray bottles of what?"

"Red Juice and Blue Juice," I said. "Those are the cleaners."

I waited to see if he was strong enough to hear about Tile Juice and the special mop, called a Shmop, that a person could clean ceilings, wood floors and linoleum with. But he was still mulling over the various juices.

"Why is one juice red and one juice blue?"

"Who knows?" I said. "It just works best that way."

I could see he wasn't ready for the full impact. No need to try to introduce him to the idea of the feather duster made of 100 percent ostrich down; the 20 all-cotton cleaning cloths; and the specially designed 10-inch plastic toothbrush (for those hard-to-reach areas around the faucets). Maybe another time I could explain the special cleaning tray I'd been needing, and the tile brush with its angled bristles.

Suddenly I noticed everyone else had left the theater. I patted him on the arm and tried to give a reassuring smile.

"It won't be so bad to have a clean house," I said. "You might like it."

Nothing More
Rewarding

The Coogles' Meow

Life hasn't been the same at our house since we started chasing coogles.

We didn't know about the coogles for a long time. We thought they were two rather ordinary, if opinionated housecats, who occasionally went on interesting rampages with our mittens and socks.

But this was unimaginative of us. It took our 10-month-old daughter, Stephanie, to identify these furry beasts as members of the exotic coogle family.

"Coogle, coogle?" she calls after them plaintively as she crawls behind them through the house. They are the first things she inquires about when she opens her eyes in the morning—"Coogle?"—and she is relentless all day long in disrupting their hiding places: behind the chairs, in the laundry basket, under the beds.

The thing is, ever since all this coogle-chasing started, none of the rest of us seems able to think of the cats as anything else but coogles. These dignified tabby cats, who have survived eight moves, 22 kittens, two toddlers, and numerous feline disorders, are now reduced to "coogledom" in what should be their peaceful twilight years.

They're destined, I'm afraid, to live out the rest of their lives as coogles.

I've seen this kind of thing happen before. In fact, having objects in your life renamed by a baby just may be one of the perks of parenthood.

For instance, I don't think I'll ever be able to think of the snowplow as anything else except the "break." That's because, when Ben was 2 years old, he and I spent a snowy February day bleakly waiting at the window for some excitement. It was the kind of day when the coming of the snowplow would be the high point. But just as it finally arrived, I had broken down completely and was pleading, "Please give me a break!"

"Don't worry," Ben said, looking at the flashing lights. "Here comes the break now."

This renaming of experience has happened to every parent I know. And often the new names cling to an object like, well, snowflakes on a break's windshield.

For years, a couple I know have eaten "downtownhot" when they're sick of eating at home. Their son Jacob gave that name to restaurant food when he was a baby, because whenever they gave him his dinner, they said, "Hot, hot." He figured if food was "hot," then "downtownhot" must be food elsewhere.

When I was growing up, my family always called hot dogs "little rascals." This was because my sister watched "The Little Rascals" TV show, which was sponsored by a hot dog company. It took us nearly a week to figure out what she insisted on having for lunch, but once we got it, the name stuck.

She's also the one who got us calling squirrels "trenches" back when she was 4 years old. We were at the park one day when she pointed to some squirrels and asked, "Are these the kind of trenches that go on the collars of trenchcoats?"

None of this makes any sense, of course, but every family has its own code words for things, names that years later make you burst into laughter for no apparent reason.

To my friend Laurie, nostrils will always be "nozzles," cookies are "tookala" (because of a boy who took a lot of them), skunks are "stunks," and Captain Kangaroo remains "Hoppy K." She has her children to thank for these enlightening ways of looking at the world.

For years, my little brother called Kool-aid "Koo-get-it"

because someone was always having to go and get it for him. And my daughter Allison, when she was 3, gave us the true definition for Tropicana, as in the orange juice.

"They call it that," she explained solemnly, "because they have to trop the oranges up and put them in the canna."

Perhaps best, though, was Ben's word for something too big even to be discussed, except in the most grandiose terms. The word to use when "big" and "large" and even "giant-sized" won't do, is *bijantic*.

It's a word the language can't do without. When the coogles are tropping up everything in sight, and you can't get a decent little rascal in a downtownhot, then you know things are a bijantic mess.

The Moving Game

It seems we can ignore this fact no longer. We have to move.

The house we are renting has been sold, and the people who bought it have become rather attached to the idea of living in it themselves. This means that, even though they are very nice people, we will probably have to vacate the premises.

For those of you who haven't moved in a long time, let me spell out what this really means: We have to put all our possessions in yet-to-be-found boxes and load them onto a yet-to-be-found truck and take them to a yet-to-be-found house, where we have to unpack all those boxes and then try to take up our lives where we left off.

Every time I think about this, I get the urge to go to sleep.

I used to think moving was great fun, because, after all, you got to live in a new place, and it was fun to look through all the boxes you'd never unpacked from your *last* move, and for a while, at least, everything about the new house would seem neat and clean.

But I don't think that anymore. Living in this house— which was far too big for us in the first place—we have accumulated mountains of stuff. I can't imagine that cardboard-box makers, if they started working triple shifts from now until April, could possibly make enough boxes for all our junk.

This is the kind of house with so many spare rooms that

you can have a room and a half just for magazines you've already read but may someday want to look at again.

We even have a room devoted to cast-off baby furniture, and a room where children put clothes sent by well-meaning relatives who don't know the current styles.

A *good* person right now would be sorting through all these items and throwing out 97 percent of them.

But I just keep yawning.

A *medium*-good person would be combing the real estate ads for a rental house that lists something like: 4 Brs, FP, w/w cpt, Half-Read Magazine Room, Baby Furniture Room, and Styleless Clothing Room.

I don't want to cast blame here, but it's because of my father that I can't make myself start house-hunting. He was not a mystical man, but he always claimed that perfect houses showed up when people really needed them.

All you had to do, he said, was to write a list of all the qualities you wanted in a house, and then sit back and wait.

No kidding.

When he and my stepmother were about to be married, they wrote down their list of house requirements. It started routinely enough: a fireplace, four bedrooms, screened porch, big backyard, lots of closet space.

But by the time they got down to items 27 and 28, my father was getting a bit whimsical. It should be near a river, he said, and have a brick sidewalk out front, and—well, a tree growing out of the living room ceiling.

"What?" said my stepmother-to-be. "You mean, a live tree *growing inside the house?*"

That's what he meant, all right. "It's always been a dream of mine," he said.

They wrote it down, laughing, because of course no house could ever have that.

But guess what? A few days later, a realtor called with a house to show them. She had the same first name as my stepmother and the same last name as my father, and the house she wanted to show them had been on the market a long time.

"No one seems to want it because it's too close to the river, it has a sidewalk made of red brick, and some idiot built the house with a tree growing right out the living room ceiling," said the realtor.

"We'll take it," said my father.

They lived there for 20 years—long enough to see the river overflow many times, the brick sidewalk disintegrate, and the living room tree shed twigs and bark onto the living room carpet over and over again.

Long enough to call themselves slaves to home repair and fix-it shops.

But who cared? They'd gotten what they'd asked for—that's what my father always pointed out, smugly.

Still, he once said, if he'd had it to do over again, he might have remembered to mention a *functioning* heating system, a foundation *without* a crack in it, and—perhaps even to wish for that tree to be just outside the house rather than in the middle of it.

Call me crazy, but if this method was good enough for my father, it's good enough for me, too. How else am I going to find a house with a Damaged Stroller Storage Closet and a Spare Bedroom for Sequined Bell-Bottoms?

The Family Kindness Act

As rules go, this is a pretty stupid one. But now that it's been made, we're stuck with it.

The two older children have to do two nice things for each other every day. Period. No excuses or postponements. No pardons.

Two nice things. Every day.

I know it's a ridiculous idea to try to legislate morality and friendliness, but there they were, in the middle of their 569th squabble the other day—something about one of them singing out of tune and the other one deliberately trying to cause a tripping accident—and out I came with it: The Family Kindness Act.

I delivered the sentence in sepulchral tones. The United States Congress should announce laws with such solemnity and sternness.

But since every rule has to have a Parental Inconvenience Aspect, I have found myself every day since then having to inquire of each child, "And what two nice things did *you* do today?"

Do you want to guess at what kinds of things I hear?

"I didn't hit him when he told me to brush my teeth."

"I was polite when she wanted to show me 16 cartwheels in a row. I just said nicely that I didn't want to see them."

"I called her to the telephone without screaming her name."

"I didn't spit in his glass of chocolate milk when he left the room."

You will be shocked to hear that, on desperate days, I have allowed these to qualify as acts of kindness. Who am I, after all, to judge the quality of someone else's good deed? My job is just to see that the rules get followed.

This is the kind of outrageous thing that happens to parents. You spend your entire adolescence and early adulthood planning to be just the opposite of your own parents. There will be no stupid notions in *your* house about dinner having to be completely devoured before it's possible to have dessert. There will be no arbitrary bedtimes, or ironclad housecleaning schedules.

Life in *your* house will flow harmoniously, and your children will be helpful and cooperative out of their sense of love and devotion to you.

And then one day you hear yourself announcing something you are calling The Rule of Juice.

The Rule of Juice is simple. It says: You will drink all the juice you pour for yourself.

My friend Alice has this basic, life-sustaining rule posted on her refrigerator, along with the other two basic rules of family living, The Rule of Tissues and the Rule of Work.

The Rule of Tissues is that you must throw out your own dirty tissues. You might think such a rule would never have to be put in writing, but let's face it: most of the time, family harmony depends upon everyone's agreement with this rule. Winter, for instance, becomes an intolerable hell if the Rule of Tissues is not enforced to the letter.

The Rule of Work—now this is an example of Alice's genius at raising kids. This rule says that when you're in a room where someone else is working, unless you can find a plausible excuse to leave the room, you have to help with the work.

Frankly, I am most impressed that Alice has managed to restrict herself to just these three basic rules, and that her household seems to run pretty smoothly, even without a Family Kindness Act. She may be checking for dirty tissues or leftover juice, but you don't find her trying to figure out if not hitting someone is just as kind as carrying their clean laundry upstairs for them.

And her children, marching off to throw out gobs of tissues while gulping down the last swallow of juice, don't stop to ask, "If something should come up today and I have the chance of doing three easy nice things, could I count one of those for tomorrow's total?"

"No," I say firmly.

"But why not?" the children whine.

I can't bring myself to explain all the rules that such a procedure would be violating: The Fairness Doctrine, the Rule of Delayed Credits, and the Rule of Aggravating Arguments, just to name a few.

So I just end up relying on my mother's old standby rule: "Because I said so."

The Chicken Pox

Plink. Plonk. Splot.

If you don't recognize these sounds, you're lucky. No doubt your household is currently free of the chicken pox.

This, you see, is what chicken pox sounds like, at least in its sprouting stage.

I ought to know. We have at least a hundred billion sprouted chicken poxes on hand right now, divided somewhat unevenly among three kids.

So I have had more than my share of opportunities lately to watch the chicken pox, *listen* to the chicken pox, and speculate about the chicken pox. In fact, I haven't had a conversation in weeks that didn't have the words "fiery, burning itching" or "calamine lotion" in it, and from the looks of things, my next few weeks will be filled with conversations about "scabs."

Great. I can't wait.

There's nothing more rewarding for a mother than to hang out with a houseful of spotty kids, saying maternal, consoling things like, "Stop that scratching! I don't care if you *do* have fiery, burning itching! You want permanent scars or something?"

One of the main things about living with the chicken pox is that you have only your kids to talk to: no one else will have anything to do with you anymore. We are now living in almost complete isolation.

The Health Department might as well have come to our

house and put up a sign saying: "These People In Here Have A Serious Contagious Disease And If You Walk Within 45 Feet Of Their House, You Will Catch This Disease And Have To Talk About Scabs and Itching For Weeks On End."

People actually cross our street to avoid coming in contact with our sidewalk.

The other day, desperate for companionship, I waved out the window to a friend of mine going by. She snatched her child out of his stroller, hid him behind her back, said, "Hi-how-are-you-hope-the-kids-are-better," and fled.

Some friend.

And when I went to my son's school to pick up some homework assignments, the secretary went into the next room and spoke to me through the door.

"But *I* don't have chicken pox," I said. I had to fight back the urge to go breathe on the papers on her desk.

"How do I know that?" she said. "Just take his homework and go."

I suppose one can't be too careful.

But people don't realize there can be bright sides to sharing a common childhood disease: it brings siblings together.

My children, who usually fight with each other as much as everybody else's kids do, now actually have found a common bond.

My heart warms when I hear them saying things like, "Which do you hate the worst: the ones between your toes or the ones between your fingers?"

"The toes," the other one answers. "Now which of *these* are worse for you: the ones inside your ears or the ones inside your throat?"

"Oh, the throat," the other will say. "Hand me those lozenges, will you?"

"I can't. My fingers are too itchy. Call Mom."

That's the other bright side. I get lots of exercise zipping back and forth with lotions, sprays, antihistamines, and acetaminophen. And periodically, when nothing is working anymore, the children let me out of the house to go rent more videos, or to plead with pharmacists for any new remedies that might have come out in the last few days.

I have become a great pal of late-night video store workers and drugstore clerks. They are my new best friends.

These are people who will talk to you about scabs and itching and the sound of chicken poxes for hours on end, if you want to, and not once will they ever jump across a desk to get away from you.

I now go jauntily into pharmacies and say, "Any new inventions this week for fiery, burning itching?"

And they say, "No, but I'm sure the scientists are working on it. Any day now."

"Great," I say. "I'll check back with you tomorrow."

And so I go back home. Back to the plonk, splot, plink of my life. Someday—soon, if the childhood medical books can be believed—the chicken pox will change sound. There will be the scritchy-scratch of scabs falling away, and the children will once again be themselves.

And then comes the best part: they can't get it again.

Spring Cleaning

There's a scary look I get on my face that sends my children running for cover.

It's not the "leave-me-alone-can't-you-see-I'm-on-the-telephone" look, which I have perfected to an art form. I can only *dream* of the day that look will clear the room.

It's not even my ultra-ferocious "where-in-the-world-did-you-leave-that-denim-jacket-I-just-paid-$75-for" look, which I have had opportunity to use all too often.

No. Apparently my all-time best scary look comes when I have noticed that it's Spring Cleaning Time.

For me, this is actually a very happy moment. There's nothing frightening about it in the least. I feel infused with energy and flooded with true ambition. It's as if, at last, I've fought my way out of a paralyzing stupor and broken through to the other side.

"Yes!" every cell of my body is screaming. "We *can* get that stuck-on grape jelly *off* the kitchen floor! We can! We can! We can!"

The children vanish into thin air.

But I track them down, bring them back to the hard realities of household dirt, and hand out their assignments. Some child psychologist or other recommends that at moments like this, you should try to make things into a Merry Game, or if you can't manage that, at least a Wonderful Challenge.

Since my children are beyond the point where "Let's sing a round of 'Row, Row, Row Your Boat' while we scrub the fingerprints off the walls" will work, I have to take the challenge route.

"How quickly," I've been known to ask, "can you put all your winter clothes into this cardboard box and race it up to the third floor? Ten minutes? Surely not *seven* minutes? *No one* has ever been able to do such a task in *seven minutes!*"

This is shameless of me, I know.

But sometimes it works.

During one of my finest moments of motherhood—this was my personal pinnacle, and I know I can never repeat it— I got a child to take apart and clean the stove merely by using words like "satisfying," "gleaming," and "the lovely aroma of pine-scented cleaner."

Since then, however, those words have taken on an ugly connotation, and to speak them in that child's presence is to invite insurrection.

Now, when it's Spring Cleaning Time—and let's face it, this is a traditional springtime sport—I have to use other, less pleasant methods to get the help I know I deserve.

Sometimes I even have to use the most powerful weapon in the Motherhood Arsenal: guilt.

I don't have to outline for you what that means. Everybody knows what a mother says at times like this. Or, if she's really an expert guilt wielder, what she *doesn't* say.

Haven't we all come upon our mother, brushing a wisp of hair out of her face while she hunkers down to scrub *our* grape jelly off the kitchen floor? Or wearily stripping the sheets off *our* bed?

Without divulging any of my own trade secrets, I just want to say that *that's* the sort of thing I'm talking about.

It's good for up to two days of steady cleaning from children, if you do it just right.

But this year I may not need to gear up for the Really Big Guilt Trips. My friend Randolph has had an epiphany of sorts, and he claims no one ever needs to go through this type of thing again.

He hired a cleaning service.

People now actually come to his house once a week and

vacuum the rugs—even behind the couch—and scrub the bathtub and wash the walls, or anything else he doesn't want to clean.

It took some getting used to. The first few times they came, Randolph cleaned right along with them, making pleasant conversation, as if they needed encouragement to plow their way through his household dirt.

But the third time, he said, he had a realization: "Hey! These aren't my *parents*!" And he took a glass of wine out to the backyard and rested. He tended to his spiritual life, he said.

One of his first major spiritual discoveries was that the hum of the vacuum and the running of water are thrilling sounds when heard from outdoors.

I like this concept. I like it a lot.

Not that I'm ready for it, you understand. Having someone else come in and deal with your own household problems is a big step, and I'm not sure I could handle it without first going on a major cleaning binge myself.

Besides, where would I be without at least one facial expression that terrifies the kids?

Lights Out

A wonderful thing happened to our family the other night. The power went out at our house.

Normally, I know, this isn't such a great thing. I had always thought of electricity as one of our more necessary conveniences.

I may have been wrong.

There we were, having one of those Sunday evenings when the entire family was being driven crazy by the existence of everybody else. It had been raining all day long, and people were jumping down each other's throats if you so much as breathed funny.

I myself was wondering how I ever got mixed up with this bunch of people and was quietly trying to figure out how far out of town I could get on the $38.59 I had in my savings account.

And then—pfffft.

That, in case you don't know, is the sound of power going out.

For a minute, nobody moved. It was like being in one of those sensory deprivation chambers—no noise, no light. Just blankness.

My first thought was that my check to pay the electric bill had probably gotten lost in the mail, and who knew when the electric company would manage to turn the power back on— probably three days later—and what in the world were they thinking, turning people's power off on Sunday night anyway? Was there no mercy in the world?

But no. It was because of a storm. Nobody had power. The entire neighborhood had gone dark.

The first thing that happens when the power goes off is that you instantly can't remember where there are any candles, matches or flashlights.

Someone thought they had seen a Coleman lantern in the garage. Someone else remembered there was a log on the back porch that we could put in the fireplace. Matches just might be on the shelf near the door, where they were left after the last time we lit the barbecue.

Too bad there was no light to go looking for these things.

People started groping their way along the walls, making sure to trip over the open dishwasher door. I personally stepped in the cat's water dish three or four times, and Stephanie, who is 5, was in charge of running into the door jambs as many times as possible.

But finally we managed to get matches and candles together in the same room, and then, suddenly, there was a fire blazing in the fireplace, and people remembered where they had stashed flashlights.

And then—well, an odd thing happened. Maybe it had to do with the fact that the glow of the candlelight didn't extend over to the kitchen sink, which was still piled high with dirty dishes, or to the homework left undone on the dining-room table. The radio station we'd been arguing about was silent.

Everybody kind of settled into another kind of evening.

The two older kids, sworn enemies only moments before, sat down to work on a weird designer candle, trying to design a wax drainage system that would keep the thing from always going out.

My husband, rediscovering man's connection to fire, started looking for things that could possibly be incinerated in the fireplace.

Stephanie did her famous Flashlight Dance, which involved leaping around the room and shining lights in our faces.

And then out came the sheet music.

Now, none of us can sing at all and usually trying to sing together is a complete disaster. But it turned out we could sing great when there wasn't any electricity.

We started out on "Somewhere Over the Rainbow" and "Chantilly Lace," and hours later, when we got around to "New York, New York" and "The Impossible Dream," we had to stand up and flail our arms in the air for the full effect.

You *cannot* sing "The Impossible Dream" without standing on tiptoe.

The fire was a tiny cinder barely glowing in the fireplace, so we huddled around the flashlight to belt out the last bars of "New York, New York." It was after midnight, and I felt as if a piano bar was closing down for good.

The power came on at 1:43 a.m. I know because suddenly I was lying in my bed, flooded with light. The stereo and TV were blaring in another part of the house. The washer and dryer were going full steam.

I got up and turned out the lights in the children's rooms. And I actually smiled.

Turn the page for an excerpt from

SLEEPING THROUGH THE NIGHT
... and other lies

Available in hardcover from
St. Martin's Press!

So you did it. You went and made yourselves a baby.

By now you've probably figured out how it happened. Oh sure, there was the sex. But you'd done that before without any babies getting started. This time, though, something mysterious and huge happened—egg and sperm actually introduced themselves to each other, shook hands, and then moved in together—and somehow all your vague ideas of *someday* have turned into *right now*.

Welcome to the Parent Club.

Perhaps you were sick of people saying, "So when are you guys going to have a kid, anyway?" Or maybe you suddenly noticed that when you were out in public, you could barely pay attention to what anybody was saying because you were so busy gazing at strangers' red-cheeked toddlers dozing in their strollers. And you couldn't help it; you'd stare at the parents, checking them out for signs of premature wear and tear, and find yourself relieved if it seemed they were still able to walk up-right.

Or maybe—and this happens more than you'd think—pregnancy just sort of started on its own, as though the baby itself issued a policy statement: "Attention, People I Have Chosen As Parents: I have waited in the World of Ideas for just about as long as I can stand. I will now be making an appearance on Earth in approximately nine months. P.S. I can make do with your spare room, but you'll have to get all that junk out of there. And by the way, we up here in the World of

Ideas found it very amusing that you thought that diaphragm didn't have any holes in it."

However it happened, one day your time of childlessness simply ran out, and here you are: a couple with a kid.

On the one hand, you've probably realized that if the two of you can survive pregnancy and everyone's horror stories about childbirth, you can probably survive anything, even parenthood.

But then there's the other hand, that voice in your ear that's always too happy to remind you how incompetent you've always been in life. It's there to remind you how badly you did, in fact, with that stupid experiment in junior high, where you had to carry around a raw egg for a week without letting it drop—and how you went through ten eggs before you finally got the idea of hard-boiling the thing so it could survive to be two weeks old.

By now it's occurred to you that if you try to hard-boil the baby, the authorities will come. And that besides feeding it and keeping it moderately clean, there's not an equivalent thing you can do for a baby to make sure it lives. Or doesn't get hurt. Or makes it through seventh grade unscathed. Or even learns how to roll over.

To make matters worse, it seems that everywhere you turn, some expert or other is announcing that the first three years of life are so wildly important that a person's whole life, future earnings, and chances of going to the senior prom are all set in place during the precise time period when you, as parents, are as freaked out as you've ever been in your life. There's this nagging little feeling, supported, I'm afraid, by everyone from your parents to the federal government and the National Institutes of Health, that you could really Get It Wrong and screw up the next generation royally. You, in fact, and your buddies who also may someday start procreating, could be personally responsible for the downfall of Western Civilization. Thanks to the way you've been living your life and are likely to be raising your child, human beings will most likely forget how to walk erect and simply turn into blobs, on their way, evolution-wise, toward being sea dwellers again.

But here's the truth: No one has ever felt remotely mentally healthy enough to raise a kid, and everybody gets it wrong every day. And even though the first three years *are* hair-raising and, yes, also extremely important, chances are your sense of good will—the same sense of good will that got you your life and your jobs and each other—can get you through. Remember this: Nobody—not even the head of the National Institute of Pediatric Health and Baby Management, if there were such a thing—knows what the hell to do when it's the middle of the night, and the kid is screaming and you've tried feeding, you've tried burping, you've tried walking, and you've tried changing diapers. You've even turned on the stereo, turned up the thermostat, turned *down* the thermostat, invented forty more verses to "I Found a Peanut" and now you're ready to consider alcoholic beverages all around, only the kid isn't twenty-one yet, and you're sure you'll get arrested.

Here are the crazy things people will tell you, and they are all true:

Sometimes turning on the clothes dryer works.

Sometimes walking very fast while singing the words to your high school fight song works.

Sometimes wrapping the baby's feet in a blanket helps.

Sometimes not eating garlic for a while will prevent other incidents like that, but probably not retroactively for this time.

But sometimes—I can't lie to you—you just have to stay up all night, holding onto this miserable little person, and all you can come away with is the knowledge that when the sun comes up, it doesn't get light all at once, but just kind of gradually gets lighter and lighter gray until you can start to notice things like flowers and lawn furniture and the individual leaves on the trees.

And that's when you realize the baby is asleep, and that you're most likely going to live through this time in your life.

Especially if you can laugh.

In fact, *definitely* if you can laugh.

Home from the hospital

Coming home from the hospital is not at all like leaving for the hospital. For one thing, the one who actually gave birth no longer has to stop every few minutes to lean against the wall and say, "Hee hoo hee hoo," while the other searches through the bag to make sure there are enough tennis balls and sour lollipops—and to ask again what the hell tennis balls and sour lollipops have to do with having a baby in the first place.

All that is over. You have now brought the tennis balls and lollipops *back* home. (My opinion is that they were to let the hospital staff see if you're the submissive type who will bring absolutely anything they suggest that you pack. I'll bet no one even did so much as one volley with the balls.)

There's a sense of huge relief, walking in your front door again, bringing along the new family member you made. The main thing is that nine months of craziness is now officially over, and even though neither you nor your husband has any freaking idea what's about to happen to your lives, at least one thing is certain: Nobody is living inside of anybody else's body anymore. Everybody's responsible for taking in food and oxygen. And someday, you feel certain, you'll even be able to walk over to your closet and pick out something to wear that doesn't have a pregnancy bulge to it.

Many people think the Moment of Homecoming is a good

time to go climb right into that bed you've missed and get your recovery well under way. Still other, more neurotic types would say this is an excellent time to turn on your workout tape and start flattening your stomach. It isn't.

This is a good time to start planning your strategy for living through the next few days.

The visitors are storming the gates

When you first bring a new baby home, it's unbelievable how many people are going to drop everything in their own lives and come to see it. People who wouldn't have gone to the trouble of crossing the street to say hello to you a few weeks ago are going to insist on "running by for a quick minute, just to get a look at the baby." There's something about a new member of the species that gets the whole planet in the mood to drive over to its house and get a bead on it.

Some of these people you will want to see, and some you will not. Some of them, in fact, will be your relatives, whom it is difficult to discourage and still maintain the kind of civility that will ensure tranquil holidays from now on.

The important thing to remember is that anyone who comes over should be willing to do some work before leaving. I know, I know. You might not be the type who *wants* your old elementary school chums taking out the trash for you—but think of this: It gives them a sense of purpose while they're visiting, *and* it keeps you from having to lug your postpartum selves to the garbage can later.

Putting visitors to work is a very tricky proposition, but it can be managed. The important thing to remember is that the new parents—that's you guys—are exhausted and deserve all the help you can get. After all, you just went through hours and hours of labor together, not to mention the nine-month construction project you've been involved in. Besides that, at least one of you is probably *lactating*. And your hormones are rampaging. You need to lie in bed and gaze at your baby, and if other people want to be there watching you do that, they should be doing two things: agreeing with you whole-heartedly that *this* is the All-Time Most Adorable Baby There Ever Was, and then, when they are done with this agreeing, they should be fixing you some dinner, or at least a nice glass of lemonade.

You will know that things are going very badly indeed if you find yourself in the kitchen serving the guests. Do not let this happen. If you find yourself with a tray in your hands, what works every time is to double over suddenly, closing your eyes for just a second. Everyone will remember that you are in a delicate condition, and they—if they are any kind of friends at all—will insist you go back to bed while they take over the refreshment portion of the visit.

Worst of all, though, is if you are in the kitchen, fixing them some tea, and they are telling you that your child seems to have an odd little point to his head. That, I would think, would be grounds for immediate eviction.

Even when things are going swell, it's good to have a plan to clear the room, if you should suddenly get sick of every-body and want to be alone with your baby. I have found that launching into a description of the birth process itself will normally scare away any men, elderly people, and childless women who might be visiting, especially if you use a few key phrases, like "bloody show," "mucous plug," or "meconium in the amniotic fluid." This method generally won't work with women who have had babies themselves; indeed, such teasing details will probably launch them into a Gruesome Birth Stories Competition.

Fortunately there's something that works even better with women who've had children. All you have to do is whisper, "I'm soooo tired," and they'll most likely take it upon them-selves in the name of sisterhood to clear the room on your be-half. Women forever after remember the kind of tiredness that comes after they've pushed a seven-pound object out of their body, and they won't be the ones to suggest that maybe you could get up and spiff the place up a little, and while you're at it, put on a pot of tea.

Take advantage of this situation while you can. And when

the guests are getting their coats and leaving, it doesn't hurt to smile sweetly and ask if they wouldn't mind taking a bag or two of garbage on their way out.

If you can't say cheese, at least you can run

Unbelievable as it may seem, some people *aren't* coming to visit you. It may seem as though everyone you've ever spoken to or passed in the grocery store is there, but in fact, some people in your life can't, due to circumstances beyond their control, make it to your house.

They are on the telephone begging you for photographs.

It is safe to say that never again in your life will there be so much need for photographs—starting on Day One. Here you are, leaking from most of your orifices and suddenly in charge of a hairless creature that looks as though it could start throwing its weight around at any moment, and your relatives are claiming that every hideous moment you're going through must be documented photographically. Someday, if the world keeps going the way it is and classes are held on every subject imaginable, Lamaze instructors will hold a separate eight-week session on How to Take Great Baby Photos, and home-care agencies will send out photographers along with visiting nurses.

Face this fact right now: Friends and relatives are going to expect all kinds of photographic records coming from your household in a practically continuous stream. You will never be able to keep up with the demand. It's best if you accept right from the beginning that you can't do it and that you develop a thick skin when all your relatives are screaming at you.

I myself have a Postal Disorder, meaning that I can't ever seem to get things to the post office in any kind of timely manner whatsoever. And, as we all know, getting pictures to relatives is lots more complicated than simply getting to the post office; first there is the film-buying project, then the taking of the photos, then taking the film in to get developed, then picking it up, then getting copies made, writing the little notes, finding the address book, writing out the envelopes— and only then do you get to the post office part, which by then anyone would be too exhausted to think of.

In our house, we have pictures of all three of the children coming home from the hospital for the first time, and I have to confess to you now: Not one of these pictures was from the Actual Homecoming.

I'm afraid they were all staged reenactments, some as many as three or four days later, or perhaps even weeks later, who knows? We took the damn picture whenever it happened that we could both locate the camera *and* manage to have at least two of us in dry, clean clothing that didn't have some kind of digested or undigested milk on it. At least we got to it before it was time to take the First Day of Kindergarten picture, and sometimes that's all that a person can ask of herself. (A hint, though: If the baby has lost that identifiable newborn scrawniness or is, say, able to walk, you should take the Hospital Homecoming picture from a very great distance.)

I find it helps if you do manage to take the Standard Baby Photos That Show That You Really Did Come up with an Actual Kid. There are some pictures that simply must be taken, or your friends and relatives will have a tough time forgiving you, and you'll be forever spending Thanksgiving dinners with them trying to justify your lapse in competence. These are almost de rigueur:

- Coming through the front door for what you will forever after claim was the first time.
- The first bath.
- The moment *after* the first bath, when the towel was draped adorably over the baby's head. (This is to prove that all three of you made it through the bath.)
- The baby swinging in the baby swing. (Keep in mind that newborns in a baby swing often look as though their necks are broken, and you don't want your relatives calling to yell at you about infant posture, so

you'll have to prop the baby in a pseudoupright position and then snap the picture within the first five seconds before he slumps down again.

- The baby screaming. (Don't ask me why people want this; I think it might be because it proves that you really did have a real, genuine baby and aren't just posing with some plastic doll or something. Surely you've noticed that dolls are never posed in the screaming position.)
- The baby sleeping—preferably on the father's chest.
- The baby nursing. (This is one of those keepsake pictures that for years will make everyone, including you, say, "Ahhhh," at the sight of the baby's round little head nestled so softly against the mountain of your breast. Some things to keep in mind in taking this picture: make sure it's not at the moment of the milk letting down, when you're liable to be gritting your teeth and saying "Yikes!" instead of looking like the radiant Madonna you wish to portray. The facial expression that accompanies the word "Yikes!" is probably not something you want in the baby book for years to come.

You will doubtlessly come up with many more pictures that beg to be taken; I've only attempted to mention the time-honored classics. But let me caution you that there are some pictures you must never take, at the risk of alienating your spouse, bigtime.

Pictures You Must Never Ever Take

- Pictures where either adult of the household is crying.
- Artistic "mood" photos that show dirty dishes, screaming baby, half-opened bathrobe, and despairing expressions.
- Those that show illegal activities, such as letting the baby ride in your arms in the car instead of the car seat.

I once personally engineered a merger, you know

Like any other new skill you're learning, parenthood takes some practice. And there are going to be some mistakes. Not really horrible mistakes, certainly, but things you definitely will want to improve upon as you go along. For instance, once I was very industriously bathing my two-week-old baby in the kitchen sink. So intent was I on making sure I was truly cleaning off all the various poopish areas that I didn't realize, until I heard the sputter, that I had her turned upside down—and the top of her head was submerged in the water. This, I could see right away, was not an award-winning bath experience. The Mother of the Year people would have crossed my name right off the list, I'm sure.

This is the kind of thing I'm talking about. No great harm was done; she didn't even turn out to be afraid of the water later in life. But still, we both had to go sit down for a long time after that incident. I don't know about her, but my legs were definitely made of rubber, and I had to work really hard to think of a good excuse to explain to her why that happened.

You see, I think it's important that the baby think that *you* know what you're doing. For a while, you may have to fake this, although I have always been afraid that, because they live so much on the sensory level, babies will pick up any vibe of fakery I might put out. (This is mainly because I lived in California when my first baby was born. By the time I had the other two in Connecticut, years later, it had fortunately become illegal to use the words *sensory level* and *vibe* in the same sentence, so I didn't worry about that anymore.)

Anyhow, I think it's a good plan to start in right away telling the baby all the things you've accomplished in your life. They don't care a great deal about mergers and real estate transactions just yet, but they pick up on the note of pride in your voice, and I think when they're out with the other babies in the strollers they can hold their heads high. Assuming they're at that physical stage, of course.

I have even been known to make little speeches. "You may think that because I got the diaper on backwards that first day that I'm some sort of incompetent wuss," I once told a skeptical baby. "But I want you to know that I have been on this planet so long that I can remember when diapers didn't even *have* tapes. In the old days, if someone did a diaper the wrong way, chances were good that someone was going to get stuck with a pin, probably either you or me. At least with tapes there are no lacerations."

A baby will be awed by this kind of information. I also found it helpful at times to address their fears directly. "I know there were a few bad moments with that bath the other day when you were thinking you might go right under the water," you might say. "But really, it was my first offense. I've been taking baths myself for decades without any ill consequences, and I'm sure we'll manage just fine from now on. By the way, did you know that I can type ninety-five words a minute, and I once single-handedly changed a tire on the highway?"

A day may come when it seems your credibility is particularly low. At that time, point out that *you* are the one who knows where the food comes from—particularly if it's true that your own body is so intelligent it happens to be *making* it on demand. I mean, this is an amazing feat right in itself, and the baby should be impressed as hell by this. I have had to explain on occasion to the baby that I was as surprised as he was that my body had this particular talent. "Before you came along, these were just ornamental, and now just look at how competent they are!"

I have several friends who believe that they got babies who slept through the night before most other people's babies did simply because they spoke with such authority on the need for sleep.

My friend Jennifer denies this now, but I clearly remember her saying to me when her first child was six months old: "I simply showed the baby that I was *the* resident sleep authority, and that I happened to know that humans slept when it was dark and got up when it was light, and that was that. No discussion."

The fates took swift revenge on such a statement, and subsequently sent Jennifer two babies who didn't buy that whole sleep authority stuff. They exposed her for what she really was all along with that first child: merely lucky.

If you should happen to have been issued one of the babies who is a child prodigy when it comes to sleeping through the night, then I think it would be best all around if you didn't brag about it to other people. Not that *you* would ever brag, of course, but there is a temptation to think that such good fortune might have been due to something wonderful you did. But believe me, if you mention this too loudly in public, you'll end up with a kid who isn't fully toilet trained until he's a freshman in high school.

The name game

One of the main things you'll find yourself doing during the first few days is thinking about the baby's name. Okay, *regretting* the baby's name. It's such a huge responsibility having to give this person the name she'll be stuck with for the rest of her life, and if you have any tendency at all toward brooding, you can hardly find a better topic to brood over than why you caved in to pressure and chose that particular name. Even if you thought you loved it, you'll find that just the act of saying it over and over again the first few days makes you think you might hate it after all.

I have hardly met any postpartum person who wasn't determined to go to the courthouse as soon as possible and do whatever was necessary to get a new name for the kid, even if she'd been calling the baby his potential new name all through fetushood. This is because you look down at this scrawny, red-faced little person and you can't imagine that he'll ever grow into being a Herbert Francis III, which you've just declared him to be. You've obviously turned your child into some kind of joke.

The truth is that some names just look ridiculous on new babies. They obviously belong to people from another generation. This is why nicknames happen. You should rest assured that whatever name you have chosen, other people are going to take over and call your kid something else altogether: Goober or Corky or Stretch, or something like that.

You'd like to take a few days to get to know the baby before saddling it with a name. But the hospital can't deal with that. Soon after you've given birth, the nurse comes in with that little form and asks for the name. If you have no idea, you feel just the tiniest bit like an idiot. As though you missed the introductions in the delivery room or something.

You feel like saying, "I'm sorry, there was so much going on that I didn't quite catch the name. If you'd just go in the nursery and ask him, I'd be so grateful."

There's a lot of pressure, no doubt about it. When the nurse came in to accost my friend Leslie and get a name for the baby, Leslie said the only name in the whole world she could ever remember hearing was Hermione. All the other names had been mysteriously erased from her brain tapes, as though she were in an episode from *The Twilight Zone* or something. Hospitals have that effect on some people. She was about to cave in and just name the baby Hermione, come what may, when her husband happened to show up. He had a few brain cells intact, enough to remember that they both liked the name Andrea, and so they did not have to go to the courthouse the next week and get things put right.

When I was in the hospital, having had my first child, my husband and I couldn't think of a single name for him. The name we'd been calling him throughout the pregnancy had suddenly soured on me after nine months of saying it to everyone. I was sitting in bed one day, reading the baby name book and worrying that the hospital staff wasn't going to let me go home until I picked out *something*, when the nurse's aide said she had the perfect name for me.

"It's the name I picked up for my son, and I've never been sorry," she said.

I picked up the pen, ready to write.

"Socrates Euphrates," she said proudly.

I picked up the baby name book again. I'd made it as far as

the Bs, and suddenly the name Benjamin looked absolutely wonderful. It was the most beautiful name in the world, and why hadn't I realized this before?

"Benjamin!" I told his father. "Let's call him Benjamin!"

All our friends and family agreed this was a splendid decision—which is a rarity indeed. It was the Name That Had Everything: style, heft, even a decent nickname.

Three weeks later, at the Lamaze class reunion, I discovered that six baby boys had been born. They were all named Benjamin. The four girls were Jennifer.